Knit Your Own Cat

To our families, who made all the right
noises when we showed them each new cat.

Black Dog & Leventhal Publishers
Hachette Book Group
1290 Avenue of the Americas
New York, NY 10104

www.blackdogandleventhal.com

First Edition: February 2012
10 9 8 7 6

Black Dog & Leventhal Publishers is an
imprint of Hachette Books, a division of
Hachette Book Group. The Black Dog &
Leventhal Publishers name and logo are
trademarks of Hachette Book Group, Inc.

The Hachette Speakers Bureau provides a
wide range of authors for speaking events.
To find out more, go to
www.HachetteSpeakersBureau.com or call
(866) 376-6591.

The publisher is not responsible for
websites (or their content) that are not
owned by the publisher.

Library of Congress Cataloging-in-
Publication Data available upon request.

ISBN-13: 978-1-57912-893-7

Knit Your Own Cat

Easy-to-Follow Patterns for 16 Frisky Felines

Sally Muir and Joanna Osborne

BLACK DOG
& LEVENTHAL
PUBLISHERS
NEW YORK

Contents

Introduction

Cats are the planet's most popular pet—there are 500 million domestic cats. We are a world of cat lovers, although with some exceptions. Genghis Khan, Hitler, Mussolini, and Napoleon Bonaparte are all reputed to have been cat haters—draw your own conclusions. The knitted cat has many of the advantages but none of the drawbacks of the live version. The knitted feline, like the real thing, will sit around looking beautiful and accept your devotion graciously, but it won't claw the furniture, climb the drapes, or bring in half-dead animals and deposit them at your feet.

Our patterns are for all levels of skill; try starting with a one-color cat, such as the Burmese, Devon Rex, Kittens, Black Cat, or British Shorthair. Once you are confident, move onto the Siamese, Black & White, Turkish Van, Abyssinian, Tortoiseshell, and Ragdoll, and then tackle the trickiest—the Persian, Tabby, Maine Coon, Orange, and Bengal. Read through the hints section on page 140 before you start, as the suggestions given will make your cat-knitting easier.

Most domestic cats aren't pedigree, so rather than covering a lot of different breeds of cat, we have chosen a selection—some pedigree, some not—and shown them in different poses. We have tried to make our cats as realistic as possible, but do feel free to make our patterns your own. Change the colors and size, or make the cats fatter or thinner, taller or shorter. Leave the tail off if you have a Manx or Bobtail cat, fold down the ears for a Scottish Fold, and make considerably shorter legs for a Munchkin.

You can make bigger cats if you prefer using thicker yarn and larger needles, and you don't have to stick to the materials that we suggest—you can use any yarn that you have lying around. The stitches used to knit the cats are fairly basic—you don't have to be an expert knitter—and the cats are small and so can be made fairly quickly.

We really want you to enjoy making these cats. Knit your own beloved or the cat you have always wanted but are allergic to; re-create the cat you had as a child or make one for a friend whose cat has died (but who doesn't want to have it stuffed); knit one cat or make them all and be a knitting Pussy Galore.

Joanna and Sally

Long-
haired

Persian

Very unusual looking, the Persian is often considered the villain's accessory. James Bond's arch enemy, Blofeld, head of SPECTRE, is seen in four Bond movies stroking his nameless white Persian cat. This has so captured our imagination that Persian-stroking has become shorthand for evil—see Austin Powers movies. On the other hand, Florence Nightingale owned 60 cats during her lifetime, including many Persians, that she often named after famous contemporaries—she had a Mr. Disraeli, a Mr. Bismark, and a Mr. Gladstone.

Persian

To create the magnificent coat, the Persian is knitted in double mohair with uncut loop stitch.

Measurements

Length: 7in (18cm)
Height to top of head: 4¾in (12cm)

Materials

- Pair of US 2 (2¾mm) knitting needles
- 4 spare US 2 (2¾mm) knitting needles or small stitch holders or safety pins
- 1¼oz (25g) of Rowan Kidsilk Haze in Cream 634 (cr) used DOUBLE throughout
- Tiny amount of Rowan Cashsoft 4ply in Kiwi 443 (ki) for eyes
- Tiny amount of Rowan Pure Wool 4ply in Black 404 (bl) for pupils and nose
- 3 pipecleaners
- Crochet hook
- Cream sewing thread for whiskers

Abbreviations

See page 141.
See page 141 for Wrap Method.
See page 141 for Loop Stitch.

Right Back Leg

With US 2 (2¾mm) needles and cr, cast on 11 sts.
Beg with a k row, work 4 rows st st.
Row 5: K3, k2tog, k1, k2tog, k3. *(9 sts)*
Row 6: Purl.
Row 7: K2, k2tog, k1, k2tog, k2. *(7 sts)*
Work 3 rows st st.
Row 11: Inc, k5, inc. *(9 sts)*
Row 12: Purl.
Row 13: Inc, k2, inc, k1, inc, k2, inc. *(13 sts)*
Row 14: Purl.
Row 15: Inc, k2, inc, k5, inc, k2, inc. *(17 sts)*
Row 16: Purl. **
Row 17: Inc, k2, inc, k9, inc, k2, inc. *(21 sts)*
Row 18: Purl.*
Row 19: Bind off 10 sts, k to end (hold 11 sts on spare needle for Right Side of Body).

Left Back Leg

Work as for Right Back Leg to *.
Row 19: K11, bind off 10 sts (hold 11 sts on spare needle for Left Side of Body).

Right Front Leg

Work as for Right Back Leg to **.
Row 17: Bind off 8 sts (hold 9 sts on spare needle for Right Side of Body).

Left Front Leg

Work as for Right Back Leg to **.
Row 17: K9, bind off 8 sts (hold 9 sts on spare needle for Left Side of Body).

Right Side of Body

Row 1: With US 2 (2¾mm) needles and cr, cast on 2 sts, with RS facing k9 from spare needle of Right Front Leg, cast on 7 sts. *(18 sts)*
Row 2: Purl.
Row 3: K18, cast on 7 sts, k11 from spare needle of Right Back Leg, cast on 1 st. *(37 sts)*
Work 3 rows st st.
Row 7: Inc, [k1, loop 1 with 2½in (6cm) loop] to end. *(38 sts)*
Work 3 rows st st.
Row 11: Inc, [k1, loop 1 with 2½in (6cm) loop] to last st, k1. *(39 sts)*
Work 3 rows st st.
Row 15: Inc, [k1, loop 1 with 2½in (6cm) loop] to last 2 sts, k1, inc. *(41 sts)*

Work 3 rows st st.
Row 19: [K1, loop 1 with 2½in (6cm) loop] to last st, k1.
Work 3 rows st st.
Row 23: Inc, [k1, loop 1 with 2½in (6cm) loop] to end. *(42 sts)*
Row 24: P5 (hold these 5 sts on spare needle for Tail), p37. *(37 sts)*
Row 25: K9 (hold these 9 sts on spare needle for Neck), bind off.

Left Side of Body

Row 1: With US 2 (2¾mm) needles and cr, cast on 2 sts, with WS facing p9 from spare needle of Left Front Leg, cast on 7 sts. *(18 sts)*
Row 2: Knit.
Row 3: P18, cast on 7 sts, p11 from spare needle of Left Back Leg, cast on 1 st. *(37 sts)*
Work 3 rows st st.
Row 7: Inc, p36. *(38 sts)*
Row 8: [K1, loop 1 with 2½in (6cm) loop] to end.
Work 2 rows st st.
Row 11: Inc, p37. *(39 sts)*
Row 12: [K1, loop 1 with 2½in (6cm) loop] to last st, k1.
Work 2 rows st st.
Row 15: P37, inc. *(41 sts)*
Row 16: [K1, loop 1 with 2½in (6cm) loop] to last st, k1.
Work 3 rows st st.
Row 20: [K1, loop 1 with 2½in (6cm) loop] to last st, k1.
Work 2 rows st st.
Row 23: Inc, p40. *(42 sts)*
Row 24: K5 (hold these 5 sts on spare needle for Tail), [k1, loop 1 with 2½in (6cm) loop] to last st, k1. *(37 sts)*
Row 25: P9 (hold these 9 sts on spare needle for Neck), bind off.

Face
Make sure the cheeks are quite well stuffed. The eyes can be either horizontal or almond shaped.

Neck and Head

Row 1: With US 2 (2¾mm) needles and cr and RS facing, k9 from spare needle of Right Side of Body for Neck, then k9 from spare needle of Left Side of Body for Neck. *(18 sts)*
Row 2: Inc, p1, inc, p12, inc, p1, inc. *(22 sts)*
Row 3: [K1, loop 1 with 2½in (6cm) loop] to end.
Row 4: Inc, p1, inc, p16, inc, p1, inc. *(26 sts)*
Row 5: K21, wrap and turn.
Row 6: P16, w&t.
Row 7: K16, w&t.
Row 8: P16, w&t.
Row 9: K to end. *(26 sts on right-hand needle)*
Row 10: Purl.
Row 11: Inc, [loop 1 with 2½in (6cm) loop] 4 times, k16, [loop 1 with 2½in (6cm) loop] 4 times, inc. *(28 sts)*
Row 12: Purl.
Row 13: K20, wrap and turn.
Row 14: P12, w&t.
Row 15: K12, w&t.
Row 16: P12, w&t.
Row 17: K to end. *(28 sts on right-hand needle)*
Row 18: P3, [p2tog] 11 times, p3. *(17 sts)*
Row 19: K1, [k2tog] 3 times, k3, [k2tog] 3 times, k1. *(11 sts)*
Row 20: [P2tog] twice, p3, [p2tog] twice. *(7 sts)*
Row 21: K3tog, k1, k3tog. *(3 sts)*
Row 22: P3tog and fasten off.

Tummy

With US 2 (2¾mm) needles and cr, cast on 8 sts.
Beg with a k row, work 64 rows st st.
Row 65: K2tog, k4, k2tog. *(6 sts)*
Work 3 rows st st.
Row 69: K2tog, k2, k2tog. *(4 sts)*
Work 3 rows st st.
Row 73: [K2tog] twice. *(2 sts)*
Row 74: P2tog and fasten off.

Ear

(make 2 the same)
With US 2 (2¾mm) needles and cr, cast on 7 sts.
Work 4 rows st st.
Row 5: K2tog, k3, k2tog. *(5 sts)*
Row 6: Purl.
Row 7: K2tog, k1, k2tog. *(3 sts)*
Row 8: Purl.
Row 9: K3tog and fasten off.

Tail

Row 1: With US 2 (2¾mm) needles and cr and RS facing, k5 from spare needle of Left Side of Body for Tail, then k5 from spare needle of Right Side of Body for Tail. *(10 sts)*
Row 2: Purl.
Row 3: [Loop 1 with 2½in (6cm) loop] 3 times, k4, [loop 1 with 2½in (6cm) loop] 3 times.
Work 3 rows st st.
Row 7: [K1, loop 1 with 2½in (6cm) loop] to end.
Work 3 rows st st.
Row 11: [K1, loop 1 with 2½in (6cm) loop] to end.
Work 3 rows st st.
Row 15: [K1, loop 1 with 2½in (6cm) loop] to end.
Work 3 rows st st.
Row 19: [K1, loop 1 with 2½in (6cm) loop] to end.
Work 3 rows st st.
Row 23: [K1, loop 1 with 2½in (6cm) loop] to end.
Row 24: P2tog, p6, p2tog. *(8 sts)*
Row 25: K2tog, k4, k2tog. *(6 sts)*
Row 26: P2tog, p2, p2tog. *(4 sts)*
Row 27: [K2tog] twice, working a 2½in (6cm) loop on both sts. *(2 sts)*
Row 28: P2tog and fasten off.

To Finish

Sew in ends, leaving ends from bound off rows for sewing up. Using mattress or whip stitch, sew up legs starting at paw. Using mattress or whip stitch, sew along back of cat and down bottom. At head, fold in half and sew edges of nose together. Using mattress or whip stitch, sew cast on row of tummy to bottom end of cat and sew final row to nose. Ease and sew tummy to fit body. Leave a 1in (2.5cm) gap between front and back legs on one side. Roll the pipecleaners in a small amount of stuffing and bend each one into a U shape. Fold over the ends (so they don't poke out of the paws) and slip into body, one pipecleaner down front legs and one down back legs. Stuff, keeping head fairly soft, and sew up gap with mattress stitch. Mold into shape. Sew up tail. You can also use another pipecleaner inside the tail to give you more control over the tail position. Sew ears to head, leaving about 6 sts between the two ears. Using a crochet hook and 2 strands of cr yarn, on the inside of each ear make two tufts. Fold bottom of chin—where final row of tummy is attached—to about halfway up head and sew down. For the eyes, use ki yarn to sew two horizontal stitches, approx ⅜in (0.75cm) long, for each eye. With bl yarn, make a stitch across the center of each eye for pupils. For nose, use bl yarn to sew two horizontal lines as shown in photograph. For whiskers, cut 3in (8cm) strands of sewing thread and thread through cheeks, then trim.

Persian Cat Sitting

You need to be pretty proficient with loop stitch to tackle a Persian, so do practice before you begin.

Measurements
Length: 9½in (24cm)
Height to top of head: 6in (15cm)

Materials
• Pair of US 2 (2¾mm) knitting needles
• 2 spare US 2 (2¾mm) knitting needles or small stitch holders or safety pins
• 1½oz (25g) of Rowan Kidsilk Haze in Cream 634 (cr) used DOUBLE throughout
• Tiny amount of Rowan Cashsoft 4ply in Kiwi 443 (ki) for eyes
• Tiny amount of Rowan Pure Wool 4ply in Black 404 (bl) for pupils and nose
• 2 pipecleaners
• Crochet hook
• Rice or lentils for stuffing
• Transparent nylon thread for whiskers

Abbreviations
See page 141.
See page 141 for Wrap Method.
See page 141 for Loop Stitch.

Back Leg
(make 2 the same)
With US 2 (2¾mm) needles and cr, cast on 13 sts.
Work 4 rows st st.

Row 5: K4, k2tog, k1, k2tog, k4. *(11 sts)*
Work 3 rows st st.
Bind off 11 sts.

Right Front Leg
With US 2 (2¾mm) needles and cr, cast on 11 sts.
Beg with a k row, work 4 rows st st.
Row 5: K3, k2tog, k1, k2tog, k3. *(9 sts)*
Work 7 rows st st.
Row 13: Inc, k2, inc, k1, inc, k2, inc. *(13 sts)*
Work 3 rows st st.
Row 17: Inc, k11, inc. *(15 sts)*
Row 18: Purl.*
Row 19: Bind off 7 sts (hold 8 sts on spare needle for Right Side of Back).

Left Front Leg
Work as for Right Front Leg to *.
Row 19: K8, bind off 7 sts (hold 8 sts on spare needle for Left Side of Back).

Right Side of Back
With US 2 (2¾mm) needles and cr, cast on 7 sts.
Beg with a k row, work 4 rows st st.
Row 5: Inc, k6. *(8 sts)*
Row 6: Purl.
Row 7: Inc, k7. *(9 sts)*
Row 8: Purl.
Row 9: Inc, k8. *(10 sts)*
Row 10: Purl.
Row 11: Inc, k9. *(11 sts)*
Row 12: P10, inc. *(12 sts)*
Row 13: Inc, k11. *(13 sts)*
Row 14: P12, inc. *(14 sts)*
Row 15: Inc, k13. *(15 sts)*
Row 16: P14, inc. *(16 sts)*
Row 17: Inc, k15. *(17 sts)*
Row 18: P16, inc, with WS facing p8 from spare needle of Right Front Leg, cast on 1 st. *(27 sts)*
Row 19: [K1, loop 1 with 2½in (6cm) loop] to last st, k1.

Work 3 rows st st.
Row 23: Inc, [k1, loop 1 with 2½in (6cm) loop] to end. *(28 sts)*
Work 3 rows st st.
Row 27: [K1, loop 1 with 2½in (6cm) loop] to end.
Row 28: Purl.
Row 29: Inc, k27. *(29 sts)*
Row 30: Purl.
Row 31: [K1, loop 1 with 2½in (6cm) loop] to last st, k1.
Row 32: Purl.
Row 33: Inc, k28. *(30 sts)*
Row 34: Purl.
Row 35: [K1, loop 1 with 2½in (6cm) loop] to end.
Row 36: P2tog, p28. *(29 sts)*
Row 37: K27, k2tog. *(28 sts)*
Row 38: P2tog, p26. *(27 sts)*
Row 39: [K1, loop 1 with 2½in (6cm) loop] to last 3 sts, k1, k2tog. *(26 sts)*
Row 40: P2tog, p24. *(25 sts)*
Row 41: K23, k2tog. *(24 sts)*
Row 42: P2tog, p20, p2tog. *(22 sts)*
Row 43: [K1, loop 1 with 2½in (6cm) loop] to last 2 sts, k2tog. *(21 sts)*
Row 44: Bind off 4 sts, p last 2 sts, p2tog. *(16 sts)*
Row 45: K2tog, k12, k2tog. *(14 sts)*
Bind off.

Left Side of Back
With US 2 (2¾mm) needles and cr, cast on 7 sts.
Beg with a p row, work 4 rows st st.
Row 5: Inc, p6. *(8 sts)*
Row 6: Knit.
Row 7: Inc, p7. *(9 sts)*
Row 8: Knit.
Row 9: Inc, p8. *(10 sts)*
Row 10: Knit.
Row 11: Inc, p9. *(11 sts)*
Row 12: K10, inc. *(12 sts)*
Row 13: Inc, p11. *(13 sts)*

Row 14: K12, inc. *(14 sts)*
Row 15: Inc, p13. *(15 sts)*
Row 16: K14, inc. *(16 sts)*
Row 17: Inc, p15. *(17 sts)*
Row 18: Inc, k16, with RS facing k8 from spare needle of Left Front Leg, cast on 1 st. *(27 sts)*
Row 19: Purl.
Row 20: [K1, loop 1 with 2½in (6cm) loop] to last st, k1.
Work 2 rows st st.
Row 23: Inc, p26. *(28 sts)*
Row 24: [K1, loop 1 with 2½in (6cm) loop] to end.
Work 3 rows st st.
Row 28: [K1, loop 1 with 2½in (6cm) loop] to end.
Row 29: Inc, p27. *(29 sts)*
Work 2 rows st st.
Row 32: [K1, loop 1 with 2½in (6cm) loop] to last st, k1.
Row 33: Inc, p28. *(30 sts)*
Work 2 rows st st.
Row 36: K2tog, [k1, loop 1 with 2½in (6cm) loop] to end. *(29 sts)*
Row 37: P27, p2tog. *(28 sts)*
Row 38: K2tog, k26. *(27 sts)*
Row 39: P25, p2tog. *(26 sts)*
Row 40: K2tog, [k1, loop 1 with 2½in (6cm) loop] to end. *(25 sts)*
Row 41: P23, p2tog. *(24 sts)*
Row 42: K2tog, k20, k2tog. *(22 sts)*
Row 43: P20, p2tog. *(21 sts)*
Row 44: Bind off 4 sts, k to last 2 sts, k2tog. *(16 sts)*
Row 45: P2tog, p12, p2tog. *(14 sts)*
Bind off.

Head

With US 2 (2¾mm) needles and cr, cast on 22 sts.
Row 1: Inc, k1, inc, k16, inc, k1, inc. *(26 sts)*
Row 2: Purl.

Face

The sitting Persian's head is knitted separately and sewn on. If you feel it's necessary, you can always add a collar or ribbon to hide the join.

Row 3: [K1, loop 1 with 2½in (6cm) loop] to end.
Row 4: Purl.
Row 5: K21, wrap and turn.
Row 6: P16, w&t.
Row 7: K16, w&t.
Row 8: P16, w&t.
Row 9: Knit to end. *(26 sts on right-hand needle)*
Row 10: Purl.
Row 11: Inc, [loop 1 with 2½in (6cm) loop] 4 times, k16, [loop 1 with 2½in (6cm) loop] 4 times, inc. *(28 sts)*
Row 12: Purl.
Row 13: K20, wrap and turn.
Row 14: P12, w&t.
Row 15: K12, w&t.
Row 16: P12, w&t.
Row 17: Knit to end. *(28 sts on right-hand needle)*
Row 18: P3, [p2tog] 11 times, p3. *(17 sts)*
Row 19: K1, [k2tog] 3 times, k3, [k2tog] 3 times, k1. *(11 sts)*
Row 20: [P2tog] twice, p3, [p2tog] twice. *(7 sts)*
Row 21: K3tog, k1, k3tog. *(3 sts)*
Row 22: P3tog and fasten off.

Tummy

With US 2 (2¾mm) needles and cr, cast on 3 sts.
Beg with a k row, work 8 rows st st.
Row 9: Inc, k1, inc. *(5 sts)*
Work 13 rows st st.
Row 23: Inc, k3, inc. *(7 sts)*
Work 27 rows st st.
Row 51: K2tog, k3, k2tog. *(5 sts)*
Work 3 rows st st.
Row 55: K2tog, k1, k2tog. *(3 sts)*
Row 56: Purl.
Row 57: K3tog and fasten off.

Ear

(make 2 the same)
With US 2 (2¾mm) needles and cr, cast on 7 sts.
Beg with a k row, work 4 rows st st.
Row 5: K2tog, k3, k2tog. *(5 sts)*
Row 6: Purl.
Row 7: K2tog, k1, k2tog. *(3 sts)*
Row 8: Purl.
Row 9: K3tog and fasten off.

Tail

With US 2 (2¾mm) needles and cr, cast on 12 sts.
Beg with a k row, work 2 rows st st.
Row 3: [K1, loop 1 with 2½in (6cm) loop] to end.
Work 3 rows st st.
Row 7: [K1, loop 1 with 2½in (6cm) loop] to end.
Work 3 rows st st.
Row 11: [K1, loop 1 with 2½in (6cm) loop] to end.
Work 3 rows st st.
Row 15: [K1, loop 1 with 2½in (6cm) loop] to end.
Work 3 rows st st.
Row 19: [K1, loop 1 with 2½in (6cm) loop] to end.
Work 3 rows st st.
Row 23: [K1, loop 1 with 2½in (6cm) loop] to end.
Work 3 rows st st.
Row 27: [K1, loop 1 with 2½in (6cm) loop] to end.
Row 28: P2tog, p8, p2tog. *(10 sts)*
Row 29: K2tog, k6, k2tog. *(8 sts)*
Row 30: P2tog, p4, p2tog. *(6 sts)*
Row 31: [K1, loop 1 with 6in (15cm) loop] to end.
Row 32: P2tog, p2, p2tog. *(4 sts)*
Row 33: [K2tog] twice. *(2 sts)*
Row 34: P2tog and fasten off.

To Finish

Sew in ends, leaving ends from bound off rows for sewing up. Using mattress or whip stitch, sew up legs starting at paw. Using mattress or whip stitch, sew along back of cat and down 7 sts cast on at bottom. Using mattress or whip stitch, sew cast on row of tummy to bottom end of cat and sew final row to top of chest. Ease and sew tummy to fit body. Leave a 1in (2.5cm) gap on one side. Roll a pipecleaner in a small amount of stuffing and bend into a U shape. Fold over the ends (so they don't poke out of the paws) and slip into body down front legs. Stuff, adding some rice or lentils to the tummy to give weight, and sew up gap with mattress stitch. Mold into shape. Fold back leg pieces in half and sew up, stuff, and attach at beginning of tummy seam to help stabilize your cat. Sew up tail and attach to base of body. For the head, fold in half and sew edges of nose together. Stuff loosely. Using mattress or whip stitch, attach head, facing sideways, to bound off sts at neck. Sew ears to head, leaving about 6 sts between the two ears. Using a crochet hook and 2 strands of cr yarn, on the inside of each ear make two tufts. Fold bottom of chin to about halfway up head and sew down. For the eyes, use ki yarn to sew two horizontal stitches, approx ⅜in (0.75cm) long, for each eye. With bl yarn, make a stitch across the center of each eye for pupils. For nose, use bl yarn to sew two horizontal lines as shown in photograph. For whiskers, cut 3in (8cm) strands of transparent nylon and thread through cheeks, then trim.

Ragdoll

Big, beautiful, and indolent, the Ragdoll is famed for its placid temperament and tendency to go limp when picked up. A Ragdoll cat lives in the Algonquin Hotel in New York City. There have been resident cats in the Algonquin since the 1930s; all the males are called Hamlet and all the females Matilda. The BBC television program *Blue Peter* was at the center of a notorious voting scandal over the naming of their Ragdoll. The viewers' chosen name of Cookie was ignored in favor of Socks. To make amends, they later got themselves another cat and called it Cookie.

Ragdoll

The Ragdoll's loops have been cut on the body, but not the tail. Feel free to leave them all uncut.

Measurements
Length: 10¼in (26cm)
Height to top of head: 4in (10cm)

Materials
- Pair of US 2 (2¾mm) knitting needles
- 4 spare US 2 (2¾mm) knitting needles or small stitch holders or safety pins
- ¼oz (10g) of Rowan Kidsilk Haze in Cocoa 628 (co) used DOUBLE throughout
- ½oz (15g) of Rowan Kidsilk Haze in Pearl 590 (pe) used DOUBLE throughout
- Tiny amount of Rowan Cashsoft 4ply in Cherish 453 (ch) for eyes
- Tiny amount of Rowan Pure Wool 4ply in Black 404 (bl) for pupils
- Rice or lentils for stuffing
- Transparent nylon thread for whiskers
- 2 pipecleaners

Abbreviations
See page 141.
See page 141 for Wrap Method.
See page 141 for Loop Stitch.
See page 141 for Intarsia Technique.

Right Back Leg
With US 2 (2¾mm) needles and co, cast on 13 sts.
Work 4 rows st st.
Row 5: K2tog, k9, k2tog. *(11 sts)*

Row 6: Purl.
Row 7: K2tog, k7, k2tog. *(9 sts)*
Row 8: Purl.
Work 2 rows st st.
Row 11: [Inc, k1] 4 times, inc. *(14 sts)*
Row 12: Purl.
Row 13: [Inc, k1] 7 times. *(21 sts)*
Row 14: Purl.*
Row 15: Bind off 10 sts, k to end (hold 11 sts on spare needle for Right Side of Body).

Left Back Leg
Work as for Right Back Leg to *.
Row 15: K11, bind off 10 sts (hold 11 sts on spare needle for Left Side of Body).

Right Front Leg
With US 2 (2¾mm) needles and co, cast on 13 sts.
Work 4 rows st st.
Row 5: K2tog, k9, k2tog. *(11 sts)*
Row 6: Purl.
Row 7: K2tog, k7, k2tog. *(9 sts)*
Work 9 rows st st.
Row 17: Inc, k7, inc. *(11 sts)*
Work 3 rows st st.**
Row 21: Bind off 5 sts, k to end (hold 6 sts on spare needle for Right Side of Body).

Left Front Leg
Work as for Right Front Leg to **.
Row 21: K6, bind off 5 sts (hold 6 sts on spare needle for Left Side of Body).

Right Side of Body
Row 1: With US 2 (2¾mm) needles and pe, cast on 2 sts, with RS facing k6 from spare needle of Right Front Leg, cast on 20 sts, k11 from spare needle of Right Back Leg, cast on 3 sts. *(42 sts)*
Row 2: Purl.
Row 3: Inc, k41. *(43 sts)*
Row 4: Purl.
Row 5: Inc, k42. *(44 sts)*

Row 6: Purl.
Row 7: [K1, loop 1 with 1½in (4cm) loop] to end.
Row 8: Purl.
Row 9: K42, k2tog. *(43 sts)*
Row 10: Purl.
Row 11: [K1, loop 1 with 1½in (4cm) loop] to last 3 sts, k1, k2tog. *(42 sts)*
Row 12: Purl.
Row 13: K40, k2tog. *(41 sts)*
Row 14: Purl.
Row 15: [K1, loop 1 with 1½in (4cm) loop] to last 3 sts, k1, k2tog. *(40 sts)*
Row 16: Purl.
Row 17: K38, k2tog. *(39 sts)*
Row 18: Purl.
Row 19: K37, k2tog. *(38 sts)*
Row 20: Purl.
Row 21: K12 (hold these 12 sts on spare needle for Neck), k2tog, k22, k2tog. *(24 sts)*
Row 22: Bind off 2 sts, p to last 2 sts, p2tog. *(21 sts)*
Row 23: Bind off 2 sts, k to last 2 sts, k2tog. *(18 sts)*
Row 24: Bind off 2 sts, p to last 2 sts, p2tog. *(15 sts)*
Row 25: Bind off 2 sts, k1 ibos, [k1, loop 1 with 1½in (4cm) loop] to last 2 sts, k2tog. *(12 sts)*
Row 26: Purl.
Bind off.

Left Side of Body
Row 1: With US 2 (2¾mm) needles and pe, cast on 2 sts, with WS facing p6 from spare needle of Left Front Leg, cast on 20 sts, k11 from spare needle of Left Back Leg, cast on 3 sts. *(42 sts)*
Row 2: Knit.
Row 3: Inc, p41. *(43 sts)*
Row 4: Knit.
Row 5: Inc, p42. *(44 sts)*
Row 6: [K1, loop 1 with 1½in (4cm) loop] to end.

Face

Due to all the loops, you may
find it easier to sew up your
Ragdoll on the outside.

Row 7: Purl.
Row 8: Knit.
Row 9: P42, p2tog. *(43 sts)*
Row 10: [K1, loop 1 with 1½in (4cm) loop]
to last st, k1.
Row 11: P41, p2tog. *(42 sts)*
Row 12: Knit.
Row 13: P40, p2tog. *(41 sts)*
Row 14: [K1, loop 1 with 1½in (4cm) loop]
to last st, k1.
Row 15: P39, p2tog. *(40 sts)*
Row 16: Knit.
Row 17: P38, p2tog. *(39 sts)*
Row 18: [K1, loop 1 with 1½in (4cm) loop]
to last st, k1.
Row 19: P37, p2tog. *(38 sts)*
Row 20: Knit.
Row 21: P12 (hold these 12 sts on spare
needle for Neck), p2tog, p22, p2tog. *(24 sts)*
Row 22: Bind off 2 sts, k to last 2 sts, k2tog.
(21 sts)
Row 23: Bind off 2 sts, p to last 2 sts, p2tog.
(18 sts)
Row 24: Bind off 2 sts, k1 ibos, [k1, loop 1
with 1½in (4cm) loop] to last 3 sts, k1,
k2tog. *(15 sts)*
Row 25: Bind off 2 sts, p to last 2 sts, p2tog.
(12 sts)
Row 26: Knit.
Bind off.

Neck and Head

Row 1: With US 2 (2¾mm) needles and pe
and RS facing, k12 from spare needle of
Right Side of Body, then k12 from spare
needle of Left Side of Body. *(24 sts)*
Row 2: Purl.
Row 3: K18, wrap and turn.
Row 4: P12, w&t.
Row 5: K12, w&t.
Row 6: P12, w&t.
Row 7: K to end. *(24 sts on right-hand
needle)*
Row 8: Purl.

Row 9: [Loop 1 with 1½in (4cm) loop] 6 times, k12, wrap and turn.
Row 10: P12, w&t.
Join in co.
Row 11: K4pe, 4co, 4pe, w&t.
Row 12: P3pe, 6co, 3pe, w&t.
Row 13: K2pe, 8co, 2pe, [loop 1 with 1½in (4cm) loops in pe] 6 times.
Row 14: [P2togpe] 3 times, p12co, [p2togpe] 3 times. *(18 sts)*
Row 15: K2togpe, k14co, k2togpe. *(16 sts)*
Row 16: P3pe, p2co, [p2togco] 3 times, p2co, p3pe. *(13 sts)*
Row 17: K2togpe, k2pe, k5co, k2pe, k2togpe. *(11 sts)*
Row 18: P2tog, p2pe, p3co, p2pe, p2togpe. *(9 sts)*
Row 19: [K2togpe] twice, k1co, [k2togpe] twice. *(5 sts)*
Cont in pe.
Row 20: P2tog, p1, p2tog. *(3 sts)*
Row 21: K3tog and fasten off.

Tummy

With US 2 (2¾mm) needles and pe, cast on 2 sts.
Beg with a k row, work 2 rows st st.
Row 3: [Inc] twice. *(4 sts)*
Row 4: Purl.
Row 5: Inc, k2, inc. *(6 sts)*
Row 6: Purl.
Row 7: Inc, k4, inc. *(8 sts)*
Work 67 rows st st.
Row 75: K2tog, k4, k2tog. *(6 sts)*
Work 5 rows st st.
Row 81: K2tog, k2, k2tog. *(4 sts)*
Work 5 rows st st.
Row 87: [K2tog] twice. *(2 sts)*
Row 88: P2tog and fasten off.

Ear

(make 2 the same)
With US 2 (2¾mm) needles and co, cast on 7 sts.

Join in pe.
Row 1: K1co, k5pe, k1co.
Row 2: P1co, p5pe, p1co.
Rep last 2 rows once more.
Row 5: K2togco, k3pe, k2togco. *(5 sts)*
Row 6: P1co, p3pe, p1co.
Row 7: K2togco, k1pe, k2togco. *(3 sts)*
Row 8: P1co, p1pe, p1co.
Row 9: K3togco and fasten off.

Tail

With US 2 (2¾mm) and co, cast on 12 sts.
Beg with a k row, work 2 rows st st.
Row 3: [K1, loop 1 with 2½in (6cm) loop] to end.
Work 3 rows st st.
Row 7: [K1, loop 1 with 2½in (6cm) loop] to end.
Work 3 rows st st.
Row 11: [K1, loop 1 with 2½in (6cm) loop] to end.
Work 3 rows st st.
Row 15: [K1, loop 1 with 2½in (6cm) loop] to end.
Work 3 rows st st.
Row 19: [K1, loop 1 with 2½in (6cm) loop] to end.
Work 3 rows st st.
Row 23: [K1, loop 1 with 2½in (6cm) loop] to end.
Work 3 rows st st.
Row 27: [K1, loop 1 with 2½in (6cm) loop] to end.
Row 28: P2tog, p8, p2tog. *(10 sts)*
Row 29: K2tog, k6, k2tog. *(8 sts)*
Row 30: P2tog, p4, p2tog. *(6 sts)*
Row 31: [K1, loop 1 with 6in (15cm) loop] to end.
Row 32: P2tog, p2, p2tog. *(4 sts)*
Row 33: [K2tog] twice. *(2 sts)*
Row 34: P2tog and fasten off.

To Finish

Sew in ends, leaving ends from bound off rows for sewing up. Using mattress or whip stitch, sew up legs starting at paw. Using mattress or whip stitch, sew along back of cat and down bottom. Using mattress or whip stitch, sew cast on row of tummy to bottom end of cat and sew final row to nose. Ease and sew tummy to fit body. Leave a 1in (2.5cm) gap between front and back legs on one side. Roll the pipecleaners in a small amount of stuffing and bend each one into a U shape. Fold over the ends (so they don't poke out of the paws) and slip into body, one pipecleaner down front legs and one down back legs. Bend legs forward in a flat position. Stuff, adding rice or lentils for extra weight, and sew up gap with mattress stitch. Mold into shape. Sew up tail and attach to body at bottom. Sew ears to head, leaving about 3 sts between the two ears. For the eyes, use ch yarn to sew three horizontal stitches, approx ⅜in (0.75cm) long, for each eye. With bl yarn, make a stitch across the center of each eye for pupils. For nose, use bl yarn to sew two horizontal lines as shown in photograph. For whiskers, cut 3in (8cm) strands of transparent nylon and thread through cheeks, then trim. Cut loops on body; leave uncut on tail.

Maine Coon

The Maine Coon is one of the largest cat breeds.
In 2010, Stewie was named the Guinness Book of
Records Longest Cat, measuring 48½in (123cm)
from nose to tail. There is an unlikely legend that
the Maine Coon first arrived in America when
Marie Antoinette sent her beloved cats there to
escape the French Revolution—they made it, she
didn't. The Maine Coon has adapted to the climate
of North America with some flamboyant features
that we like to think wouldn't have been out of place
at Versailles—hairy toes and ears, a bushy tail, a
magnificent mane, and they can also be polydactyl
(having more than the usual number of toes).

Maine Coon

The Maine Coon is one of the more complicated cats to make, but well worth the work.

Measurements

Length including tail: 9½in (24cm)
Height to top of head: 6in (15cm)

Materials

- Pair of US 2 (2¾mm) knitting needles
- 2 spare US 2 (2¾mm) knitting needles or small stitch holders or safety pins
- 1oz (20g) of Rowan Kidsilk Haze in Wicked 599 (wk) used DOUBLE throughout
- 1oz (20g) of Rowan Kidsilk Haze in Anthracite 639 (an) used DOUBLE throughout
- ¼oz (10g) of Rowan Kidsilk Haze in Cream 634 (cr) used DOUBLE throughout
- Tiny amount of Rowan Cashsoft 4ply in Kiwi 443 (ki) for eyes
- Tiny amount of Rowan Pure Wool 4ply in Black 404 (bl) for nose
- Rice or lentils for stuffing
- 1 pipecleaner
- Crochet hook
- Black sewing thread or transparent nylon thread for whiskers

Abbreviations

See page 141.
See page 141 for Wrap Method.
See page 141 for Loop Stitch.
See page 141 for Intarsia Technique.

Back Leg

(make 2 the same)
With US 2 (2¾mm) needles and wk, cast on 13 sts.
Beg with a k row, work 4 rows st st.
Join in an.
Row 5: K2togwk, k4an, k5wk, k2togwk. *(11 sts)*
Row 6: P9wk, p2an.
Row 7: K4wk, k7an.
Row 8: P3an, p8wk.
Bind off.

Right Front Leg

With US 2 (2¾mm) needles and wk, cast on 13 sts.
Beg with a k row, work 4 rows st st.
Row 5: K2togwk, k4an, k5wk, k2togwk. *(11 sts)*
Row 6: P9wk, p2an.
Row 7: K4wk, k7an.
Row 8: P3an, p8wk.
Row 9: K11wk.
Row 10: P2wk, p4an, p5wk.
Row 11: K3wk, k4an, k4wk.
Row 12: P6wk, p5an.
Row 13: K3an, k8wk.
Row 14: P11wk.
Row 15: K2wk, k5an, k4wk.
Row 16: P6an, p5wk.
Row 17: Incwk, k9wk, incwk. *(13 sts)*
Row 18: P13wk.
Row 19: Incwk, k2wk, k6an, k3wk, incwk. *(15 sts)*
Row 20: P7wk, p8an.
Row 21: K5an, k10wk.
Row 22: P15wk.*
Row 23: Bind off 7 sts (hold rem 8 sts on spare needle for Right Side of Back).

Left Front Leg

Work as for Right Front Leg to *.
Row 23: K8, bind off 7 sts (hold rem 8 sts on spare needle for Left Side of Back).

Right Side of Back

With US 2 (2¾mm) needles and an, cast on 9 sts.
Beg with a k row, work 4 rows st st.
Row 5: Inc, k8. *(10 sts)*
Row 6: Purl.
Row 7: Inc, k9. *(11 sts)*
Row 8: Purl.
Row 9: Inc, k10. *(12 sts)*
Row 10: Purl.
Row 11: Inc, k11. *(13 sts)*
Row 12: P12, inc. *(14 sts)*
Row 13: Inc, k13. *(15 sts)*
Row 14: P14, inc. *(16 sts)*
Row 15: Inc, k15. *(17 sts)*
Row 16: P16, inc. *(18 sts)*
Row 17: Inc, k17. *(19 sts)*
Row 18: P18, inc. *(20 sts)*
Row 19: Inc, k19. *(21 sts)*
Row 20: Purl.
Row 21: Inc, [k1, loop 1 with 2½in (6cm) loop] to end. *(22 sts)*
Row 22: Purl.
Row 23: Inc, k21. *(23 sts)*
Row 24: P23, with WS facing p8 from spare needle of Right Front Leg, cast on 1 st. *(32 sts)*
Row 25: Inc, [k1, loop 1 with 2½in (6cm) loop] to last st, k1. *(33 sts)*
Join in wk.
Row 26: P4wk, p29an.
Row 27: K27an, k6wk.
Row 28: Incwk, p8wk, p24an. *(34 sts)*
Row 29: [K1, loop 1 with 2½in (6cm) loop] to end, working 20an, 14wk.
Row 30: P16wk, p18an.
Row 31: K16an, k18wk.
Row 32: P20wk, p14an.
Row 33: [K1, loop 1 with 1½in (4cm) loop] to end, working 12an, 22wk.
Row 34: P24wk, p10an.
Row 35: Incan, k7an, k26wk. *(35 sts)*
Row 36: P28wk, p7an.
Row 37: K1, [k1, loop 1 with 1½in (4cm) loop] to end, working 5an, 30wk.

Row 38: Bind off 5 sts wk, p27wk ibos, p3an. *(30 sts)*
Row 39: K2togan, k26wk, k2togwk. *(28 sts)*
Row 40: P28wk.
Row 41: [K1, loop 1 with 1½in (4cm) loop], working 6an, 20wk, to last 2 sts, k2togwk. *(27 sts)*
Row 42: P19wk, p8an.
Row 43: K2togan, k8an, k15wk, k2togwk. *(25 sts)*
Row 44: P16wk, p9an.
Row 45: K2togan, [k1, loop 1 with 1½in (4cm) loop], working 8an, 12wk, to last 3 sts, k1wk, k2togwk. *(23 sts)*
Row 46: P2togwk, p12wk, p9an. *(22 sts)*
Row 47: K2togan, k9an, k9wk, k2togwk. *(20 sts)*
Row 48: P10wk, p8an, p2togan. *(19 sts)*
Row 49: K2togan, [k1, loop 1 with 1½in (4cm) loop], working 8an, 6wk, to last 3 sts, k1wk, k2togwk. *(17 sts)*
Row 50: P2togwk, p6wk, p9an. *(16 sts)*
Row 51: K2togan, k8an, k4wk, k2togwk. *(14 sts)*
Row 52: P2togwk, p3wk, p7an, p2togan (hold 12 sts on spare needle for Head).

Left Side of Back

With US 2 (2¾mm) needles and an, cast on 9 sts.
Beg with a p row, work 4 rows st st.
Row 5: Inc, p8. *(10 sts)*
Row 6: Knit.
Row 7: Inc, p9. *(11 sts)*
Row 8: Knit.
Row 9: Inc, p10. *(12 sts)*
Row 10: Knit.
Row 11: Inc, p11. *(13 sts)*
Row 12: K12, inc. *(14 sts)*
Row 13: Inc, p13. *(15 sts)*
Row 14: K14, inc. *(16 sts)*
Row 15: Inc, p15. *(17 sts)*
Row 16: K16, inc. *(18 sts)*

Row 17: Inc, p17. *(19 sts)*
Row 18: K18, inc. *(20 sts)*
Row 19: Inc, p19. *(21 sts)*
Row 20: [K1, loop 1 with 2½in (6cm) loop] to last st, k1.
Row 21: Inc, p20. *(22 sts)*
Row 22: Knit.
Row 23: Inc, p21. *(23 sts)*
Row 24: [K1, loop 1 with 2½in (6cm) loop] to last st, k1, then with RS facing k8 from spare needle of Left Front Leg, cast on 1 st. *(32 sts)*
Row 25: Inc, p31. *(33 sts)*
Join in wk.
Row 26: K4wk, k29an.
Row 27: P27an, p6wk.
Row 28: Incwk, [k1, loop 1 with 2½in (6cm) loop] to end, working 7wk, 25an. *(34 sts)*
Row 29: P20an, p14wk.
Row 30: K16wk, k18an.
Row 31: P16an, p18wk.
Row 32: [K1, loop 1 with 1½in (4cm) loop] to end, working 20wk, 14an.
Row 33: P12an, p22wk.
Row 34: K24wk, k10an.
Row 35: Incan, p7an, p26wk. *(35 sts)*
Row 36: K1wk, [k1, loop 1 with 1½in (4cm) loop] to end, working 27wk, 7an.
Row 37: P5an, p30wk.
Row 38: Bind off 5 sts wk, k27wk ibos, k3an. *(30 sts)*
Row 39: P2togwk, p26an, p2togwk. *(28 sts)*
Row 40: [K1, loop 1 with 1½in (4cm) loop] to end in wk.
Row 41: P6an, p20wk, p2togwk. *(27 sts)*
Row 42: K19wk, k8an.
Row 43: K2togan, p8an, p15wk, p2togwk. *(25 sts)*
Row 44: K1wk, [k1, loop 1 with 1½in (4cm) loop] to end, working 15wk, 9an.
Row 45: P2togan, p8an, p13wk, p2togwk. *(23 sts)*
Row 46: K2togwk, k12wk, k9an. *(22 sts)*

Feet
You can hook yarn through with a crochet hook to make the hair between the Maine Coon's toes.

Head

The magnificent ruff is knitted separately and popped over the Maine Coon's head.

Row 47: P2togan, p9an, p9wk, p2togwk. *(20 sts)*

Row 48: [K1, loop 1 with 1½in (4cm) loop], working 10wk, k8an, to last 2 sts, k2togan. *(19 sts)*

Row 49: P2togan, p8an, p7wk, p2togwk. *(17 sts)*

Row 50: K2togwk, k6wk, k9an. *(16 sts)*

Row 51: P2togan, p8an, p4wk, p2togwk. *(14 sts)*

Row 52: K2togwk, [k1, loop 1 with 1½in (4cm) loop], working k3wk, k7an, to last 2 sts, k2togan (hold 12 sts on spare needle for Head).

Head

Row 1: With US 2 (2¾mm) needles and an, k12 from spare needle of Right Side of Body, then k12 from spare needle of Left Side of Body. *(24 sts)*

Row 2: Purl.

Row 3: Knit.

Row 4: Purl.

Row 5: K18, wrap and turn.

Row 6: P12, w&t.

Row 7: K12, w&t.

Rep last 2 rows once more.

Row 10: P12, w&t.

Row 11: K to end. *(24 sts on right-hand needle)*

Row 12: P12, inc, p11. *(25 sts)*

Join in wk.

Row 13: K10an, k1wk, k3an, k1wk, k4an, wrap and turn.

Row 14: P4an, p1wk, p3an, p1wk, p4an, w&t.

Row 15: K3an, k1wk, k1an, k1wk, k1an, k1wk, k1an, k1wk, k3an, w&t.

Row 16: P3an, p1wk, p1an, p1wk, p1an, p1wk, p1an, p1wk, p3an, w&t.

Row 17: K2an, k1wk, k3an, k1wk, k3an, k1wk, k2an, w&t.

Row 18: P2an, p1wk, p7an, p1wk, p2an, w&t.

Cont in an.

Row 19: K to end. *(25 sts on right-hand needle)*

Row 20: [P2tog] 6 times, p1, [p2tog] 6 times. *(13 sts)*

Row 21: [K2tog] twice, k5, [k2tog] twice. *(9 sts)*

Row 22: [P2tog] twice, p1, [p2tog] twice. *(5 sts)*

Bind off.

Tummy

With US 2 (2¾mm) needles and an, cast on 3 sts.

Beg with a k row, work 8 rows st st.

Row 9: Inc, k1, inc. *(5 sts)*

Work 61 rows st st.

Row 71: K2tog, k1, k2tog. *(3 sts)*

Row 72: Purl.

Row 73: K2tog, k1. *(2 sts)*

Row 74: P2tog and fasten off.

Ruff

With US 2 (2¾mm) needles and an, cast on 12 sts.

Row 1: Purl.

Row 2: [Loop 1 with 2in (5cm) loop] to end.

Work 3 rows st st.

Row 6: [Loop 1 with 2in (5cm) loop] 4 times, k2tog, turn, work on these 5 sts only.

Work 3 rows st st.

Row 10: [Loop 1 with 2in (5cm) loop] to end.

Work 3 rows st st.

Row 14: [Loop 1 with 2in (5cm) loop] to end.

Work 2 rows st st.

Hold these 5 sts on spare needle.

Rejoin yarn to rem sts, k2tog, [loop 1 with 2in (5cm) loop] to end. *(5 sts)*

Work 3 rows st st.

Row 10: [Loop 1 with 2in (5cm) loop] to end.

Work 3 rows st st.

Row 14: [Loop 1 with 2in (5cm) loop] to end.

Work 2 rows st st.

Row 17: P across all sts. *(10 sts)*

Row 18: [Loop 1 with 2in (5cm) loop] to end. *(10 sts)*
Join in cr.
Row 19: Incan, p2an, p4cr, p2an, incan. *(12 sts)*
Cont in cr.
Row 20: K12.
Row 21: Purl.
Row 22: [Loop 1 with 2½in (6cm) loop] to end.
Row 23: Inc, p10, inc. *(14 sts)*
Row 24: Inc, k12, inc. *(16 sts)*
Row 25: Purl.
Row 26: [Loop 1 with 2½in (6cm) loop] to end.
Row 27: P2tog, p12, p2tog. *(14 sts)*
Row 28: K2tog, k10, k2tog. *(12 sts)*
Row 29: P2tog, p8, p2tog. *(10 sts)*
Row 30: [Loop 1 with 2½in (6cm) loop] to end.
Row 31: P2tog, p6, p2tog. *(8 sts)*
Row 32: K2tog, k4, k2tog. *(6 sts)*
Row 33: Purl.
Row 34: [Loop 1 with 2½in (6cm) loop] to end.
Bind off.

Ear Back

(make 2 the same)
With US 2 (2¾mm) needles and wk, cast on 7 sts.
Beg with a k row, work 6 rows st st.
Row 7: K2tog, k3, k2tog. *(5 sts)*
Row 8: Purl.
Row 9: K2tog, k1, k2tog. *(3 sts)*
Row 10: P3tog and fasten off.

Ear Front

(make 2 the same)
With US 2 (2¾mm) needles and cr, cast on 6 sts.
Beg with a k row, work 5 rows st st.
Row 6: P2tog, p2, p2tog. *(4 sts)*
Row 7: Knit.

Row 8: [P2tog] twice. *(2 sts)*
Row 9: K2tog and fasten off.

Tail

With US 2 (2¾mm) needles and wk, cast on 12 sts.
Beg with a k row, work 2 rows st st.
Row 3: [K1, loop 1 with 6in (15cm) loop], working 8wk, 4an.
Row 4: P4an, p8wk.
Row 5: K8wk, k4an.
Row 6: P4an, k8wk.
Rep rows 3–6 five more times.
Row 27: As row 3.
Row 28: P2togan, p2an, p6wk, p2togwk. *(10 sts)*
Row 29: K2togwk, k5wk, k1an, k2togan. *(8 sts)*
Row 30: P2togan, p4wk, p2togwk. *(6 sts)*
Row 31: [K1, loop 1 with 2in (5cm) loop], working 5wk, 1an.
Row 32: P2tog, p2, p2tog. *(4 sts)*
Row 33: [K2tog] twice. *(2 sts)*
Row 34: P2tog and fasten off.

To Finish

Sew in ends, leaving ends from bound off rows for sewing up. Using mattress or whip stitch, sew up legs starting at paw. Using mattress or whip stitch, sew along back of cat and down bottom, including first 9 cast on stitches. Using mattress or whip stitch, sew cast on row of tummy to bottom end of cat and sew final row to nose. Ease and sew tummy to fit body. Leave a 1in (2.5cm) gap on one side. Roll a pipecleaner in a small amount of stuffing and bend into a U shape. Fold over the ends (so they don't poke out of the paws) and slip into front legs. Stuff body with lentils or rice as well as stuffing (to give extra weight) and sew up gap with mattress stitch. Mold into shape. Using an yarn, embroider separate toes. Using whip stitch, sew up and lightly stuff back legs. Attach at

very beginning of tummy seam. Sew up tail and attach to base of body. With wk yarn and whip stitch, sew front of ear to back of ear, leaving a characteristic tuft at top of ear. Sew ears to head, leaving about 3 sts between the two ears. Using a crochet hook and 2 strands of an yarn, on the inside of each ear make two tufts. For the eyes, use ki yarn to make French knots. Work each knot over 2 sts at a slight angle and wrap the yarn around the needle four times. For nose, use bl yarn to sew two horizontal lines as shown in photograph. For whiskers, cut 3in (8cm) strands of transparent nylon and thread through cheeks, then trim. Slip ruff over head and catch bound off edge to lower chest.

Turkish Van

Often referred to as the swimming cat, the Turkish Van is the only known cat that likes to get into the bath with its owner and to help with the washing up. Highly intelligent and commanding, this cat is also the David Bowie of the cat world—odd-eyed. Van, where this breed comes from in Turkey, is a few miles from Mount Ararat, where Noah's ark was said to have ended up. Susan Boyle's beloved cat Pebbles is a Turkish Van.

Turkish Van

Our Van is knitted in mohair yarn to show off his hairy coat.

Measurements
Length: 5¼in (13cm)
Height to top of head: 5½in (14cm)

Materials
- Pair of US 2 (2¾mm) knitting needles
- 4 spare US 2 (2¾mm) knitting needles or small stitch holders or safety pins
- Pair of US 2 (2¾mm) double-pointed knitting needles
- 1oz (20g) of Rowan Kidsilk Haze in Cream 634 (cr) used DOUBLE throughout
- ⅛oz (5g) of Rowan Kidsilk Haze in Brick 649 (br) used DOUBLE throughout
- Tiny amount of Rowan Cashsoft 4ply in Cherish 453 (ch) for eyes
- Tiny amount of Rowan Cashsoft 4ply in Almond 458 (al) for eyes
- Tiny amount of Rowan Pure Wool 4ply in Black 404 (bl) for pupils
- Tiny amount of Rowan Pure Wool 4ply in Powder 443 (po) for nose
- 3 pipecleaners
- Cream sewing thread for whiskers

Abbreviations
See page 141.
See page 141 for Wrap Method.
See page 141 for Loop Stitch.

Right Back Leg
With US 2 (2¾mm) needles and cr, cast on 9 sts.
Beg with a k row, work 2 rows st st.
Row 3: Inc, k1, k2tog, k1, k2tog, k1, inc. *(9 sts)*
Row 4: Purl.
Rep last 2 rows once more.*
Work 4 rows st st.
Row 11: K2, inc, k3, inc, k2. *(11 sts)*
Row 12: Purl.
Row 13: K2, inc, k5, inc, k2. *(13 sts)*
Row 14: Purl.
Row 15: K2tog, inc, k7, inc, k2tog. *(13 sts)*
Row 16: Purl.
Row 17: K2tog, inc, k2, inc, k1, inc, k2, inc, k2tog. *(15 sts)*
Row 18: Purl.
Row 19: K3, inc, k7, inc, k3. *(17 sts)*
Row 20: Purl.
Row 21: K4, inc, k7, inc, k4. *(19 sts)*
Row 22: P5, inc, p7, inc, p5. *(21 sts)*
Row 23: K6, inc, k7, inc, k6. *(23 sts)*
Row 24: Purl.**
Row 25: Bind off 11 sts, k to end (hold 12 sts on spare needle for Right Side of Back).

Left Back Leg
Work as for Right Back Leg to **.
Row 25: K12, bind off 11 sts (hold 12 sts on spare needle for Left Side of Back).

Right Front Leg
Work as for Right Back Leg to *.
Work 8 rows st st.
Row 15: Inc, k7, inc. *(11 sts)*
Row 16: Purl.
Row 17: K3, inc, k3, inc, k3. *(13 sts)*
Row 18: Purl.
Row 19: K5, inc, k1, inc, k5. *(15 sts)*
Row 20: Purl.***
Row 21: Bind off 7 sts, k to end (hold 8 sts on spare needle for Right Side of Back).

Left Front Leg
Work as for Right Front Leg to ***.
Row 21: K8, bind off 7 sts (hold 8 sts on spare needle for Left Side of Back).

Right Side of Back
Row 1: With US 2 (2¾mm) needles and cr, cast on 1 st, with RS facing k8 from spare needle of Right Front Leg, cast on 6 sts. *(15 sts)*
Row 2: Purl.
Row 3: Inc, k14, cast on 5 sts, with RS facing k12 from spare needle of Right Back Leg, cast on 1 st. *(34 sts)*
Row 4: Purl.
Row 5: Inc, k33. *(35 sts)*
Work 11 rows st st.
Row 17: K2tog, k33. *(34 sts)*
Work 2 rows st st.
Row 20: P2tog, p32. *(33 sts)*
Row 21: K2tog, k29, k2tog. *(31 sts)*
Row 22: P2tog, p29. *(30 sts)*
Row 23: K10 (hold these 10 sts on spare needle for Neck), bind off 20 sts.

Left Side of Back
Row 1: With US 2 (2¾mm) needles and cr, cast on 1 st, with WS facing p8 from spare needle of Left Front Leg, cast on 6 sts. *(15 sts)*
Row 2: Knit.
Row 3: Inc, p14, cast on 5 sts, with WS facing p12 from spare needle of Left Back Leg, cast on 1 st. *(34 sts)*
Row 4: Knit.
Row 5: Inc, p33. *(35 sts)*
Work 11 rows st st.
Row 17: P2tog, p33. *(34 sts)*
Work 2 rows st st.
Row 20: K2tog, k32. *(33 sts)*
Row 21: P2tog, p29, p2tog. *(31 sts)*
Row 22: K2tog, k29. *(30 sts)*
Row 23: P10 (hold these 10 sts on spare needle for Neck), bind off 20 sts.

Head

Our Van has unusual odd-colored almond-shaped eyes. Turn to page 140 for hints for alternative eyes.

Neck and Head

Row 1: With US 2 (2¾mm) needles and cr, k10 from spare needle of Right Side of Body, then k10 from spare needle of Left Side of Body. *(20 sts)*

Row 2: P4, p2tog, p8, p2tog, p4. *(18 sts)*

Row 3: K2tog, k14, k2tog. *(16 sts)*

Row 4: P4, inc, p6, inc, p4. *(18 sts)*
Join in br.

Row 5: K7cr, k4br, k5cr, wrap and turn.

Row 6: P3cr, p8br, p3cr, w&t.

Row 7: K1cr, k12br, k1cr, w&t.

Row 8: P14br, w&t.

Row 9: k14br, w&t.

Row 10: P14br, w&t.

Row 11: K16br. *(18 sts on right-hand needle)*

Row 12: P18br.

Row 13: K2cr, k14br, wrap and turn.

Row 14: P2cr, p10br, p2cr, w&t.

Row 15: K2cr, k4br, k2cr, k4br, k2cr, w&t.

Row 16: P3cr, p3br, p2cr, p3br, p3cr, w&t.

Row 17: K3cr, k2br, k4cr, k2br, k3cr, w&t.

Row 18: P3cr, p2br, p4cr, p2br, p3cr, w&t.
Cont in cr.

Row 19: K16. *(18 sts on right-hand needle)*

Row 20: [P2tog, p2] 4 times, p2tog. *(13 sts)*

Row 21: K3, k2tog, k3, k2tog, k3. *(11 sts)*

Row 22: P2, p2tog, p3, p2tog, p2. *(9 sts)*

Row 23: K2, k2tog, k1, k2tog, k2. *(7 sts)*
Bind off.

Tummy

With US 2 (2¾mm) needles and cr, cast on 4 sts.
Beg with a k row, work 14 rows st st.

Row 15: Inc, k2, inc. *(6 sts)*
Work 23 rows st st.

Row 39: K2tog, k2, k2tog. *(4 sts)*
Work 5 rows st st.

Row 45: Inc, k2, inc. *(6 sts)*
Work 27 rows st st.

Row 73: K2tog, k2, k2tog. *(4 sts)*
Work 9 rows st st.

Row 83: [K2tog] twice. *(2 sts)*

Tail

The tail is striped and has uncut loops. You can cut them if you want a wilder effect.

Work 3 rows st st.
Row 87: K2tog and fasten off.

Ear

(make 2 the same)
With US 2 (2¾mm) needles and br, cast on 6 sts.
Beg with a k row, work 3 rows st st.
Row 4: P2tog, p2, p2tog. *(4 sts)*
Work 2 rows st st.
Row 7: [K2tog] twice. *(2 sts)*
Row 8: P2tog and fasten off.

Tail

With US 2 (2¾mm) double-pointed needles, starting with the tip of the tail and br, cast on 3 sts.
Work in i-cord as follows:
Knit 2 rows.
Row 3: Inc, k1, inc. *(5 sts)*
Row 4: Inc, k3, inc. *(7 sts)*
Row 5: Inc, k5, inc. *(9 sts)*
Knit 4 rows.
Join in cr.
Knit 2 rows cr.
Knit 1 row br.
Row 13: K1br, [loop 1br] 7 times, k1br.
*Knit 2 rows cr.
Knit 2 rows br.
Knit 2 rows cr.
Knit 1 row br.
Row 21: K1br, [loop 1br] 7 times, k1br.*
Rep from * to * once more.
Knit 7 rows br.
Row 37: K1br, [loop 1br] 7 times, k1br.
Knit 2 rows br.
Bind off.

To Finish

Sew in ends, leaving ends from bound off rows for sewing up. Using mattress or whip stitch, sew up legs starting at paw. Using mattress or whip stitch, sew along back of cat and down bottom. At head, fold in half and sew bound off edges of nose together. Using mattress or whip stitch, sew cast on row of tummy to bottom end of cat and sew final row to nose. Ease and sew tummy to fit body, matching curves to front legs. Leave a 1in (2.5cm) gap between front and back legs on one side. Roll the pipecleaners in a small amount of stuffing and bend each one into a U shape. Fold over the ends (so they don't poke out of the paws) and slip into body, one pipecleaner down front legs and one down back legs. Fold a pipecleaner in half and slip into the head and body; this is optional but useful if you want movement in the head. Stuff, and sew up gap with mattress stitch. Mold into shape. Attach the tail as in photograph. Sew ears to head, leaving about 3 sts between the two ears. For the eyes, make elongated French knots, one eye in al yarn and one eye in ch yarn (or both eyes the same color). Work each knot over 2 sts at a slight angle and wrap the yarn around the needle five times. With bl yarn, make a stitch over the center of the French knot. Using po yarn, embroider a small nose in satin stitch. For whiskers, cut 3in (8cm) strands of sewing thread and thread through cheeks, then trim.

Short-
haired

Kittens

Everyone loves a kitten.

White Kitten

Knitting him in mohair
yarn makes the kitten
luxuriously furry.

Measurements
Length: 3½in (9cm)
Height to top of head: 4½in (11cm)

Materials
- Pair of US 2 (2¾mm) knitting needles
- 4 spare US 2 (2¾mm) knitting needles or small stitch holders or safety pins
- Pair of US 2 (2¾mm) double-pointed knitting needles
- Small amount of Rowan Kidsilk Haze in Pearl 590 (pe) used DOUBLE throughout
- ½oz (15g) of Rowan Kidsilk Haze in Cream 634 (cr) used DOUBLE throughout
- Tiny amount of Rowan Pure Wool 4ply in Powder 443 (po) for nose
- Tiny amount of Rowan Pure Wool 4ply in Sage 448 (sa) for eyes
- 2 pipecleaners
- Transparent nylon thread for whiskers
- Ribbon for neck (optional)

Abbreviations
See page 141.
See page 141 for Wrap Method.

Right Back Leg
With US 2 (2¾mm) needles and pe, cast on 13 sts.
Beg with a k row, work 2 rows st st.
Row 3: K2tog, inc, k7, inc, k2tog. *(13 sts)*
Row 4: Purl.
Change to cr.
Rep last 2 rows once more.
Work 4 rows st st.
Row 11: Inc, k11, inc. *(15 sts)*
Row 12: Purl.
Row 13: Inc, k13, inc. *(17 sts)*
Row 14: Purl.*
Row 15: Bind off 9 sts, k to end (hold 8 sts on spare needle for Right Side of Body).

Left Back Leg
Work as for Right Back Leg to *.
Row 15: K8, bind off 9 sts (hold 8 sts on spare needle for Left Side of Body).

Right Front Leg
With US 2 (2¾mm) needles and pe, cast on 13 sts.
Beg with a k row, work 2 rows st st.
Row 3: K2tog, inc, k7, inc, k2tog. *(13 sts)*
Row 4: Purl.
Change to cr.
Rep last 2 rows once more.
Work 6 rows st st.
Row 13: Inc, k11, inc. *(15 sts)*
Row 14: Purl.**
Row 15: Bind off 8 sts, k to end (hold 7 sts on spare needle for Right Side of Body).

Left Front Leg
Work as for Right Front Leg to **.
Row 15: K7, bind off 8 sts (hold 7 sts on spare needle for Left Side of Body).

Right Side of Body
Row 1: With US 2 (2¾mm) needles and cr, cast on 1 st, with RS facing k7 from spare needle of Right Front Leg, cast on 4 sts knitwise. *(12 sts)*
Row 2: P12.
Row 3: K12, cast on 3 sts, with RS facing k8 from spare needle of Right Back Leg. *(23 sts)*
Row 4: Purl.
Work 10 rows st st.
Row 15: Inc, k20, k2tog. *(23 sts)*
Row 16: Purl.
Row 17: K21, k2tog. *(22 sts)*
Row 18: P4 (hold these 4 sts on spare needle for Tail), p18. *(18 sts)*
Row 19: K16, k2tog. *(17 sts)*
Row 20: Bind off 9 sts, p to end (hold 8 sts on spare needle for Neck).

Left Side of Body
Row 1: With US 2 (2¾mm) needles and cr, cast on 1 st, with WS facing p7 from spare needle of Left Front Leg, cast on 4 sts purlwise. *(12 sts)*
Row 2: K12.
Row 3: P12, cast on 3 sts, with WS facing p8 from spare needle of Left Back Leg. *(23 sts)*
Row 4: Knit.
Work 10 rows st st.
Row 15: Inc, p20, p2tog. *(23 sts)*
Row 16: Knit.
Row 17: P21, p2tog. *(22 sts)*
Row 18: K4 (hold these 4 sts on spare needle for Tail), k18. *(18 sts)*
Row 19: P16, p2tog. *(17 sts)*
Row 20: Bind off 9 sts, k to end (hold 8 sts on spare needle for Neck).

Neck and Head

Row 1: With US 2 (2¾mm) needles and cr and RS facing, k8 from spare needle of Right Side of Body, then k8 from spare needle of Left Side of Body. *(16 sts)*

Row 2: P2tog, p12, p2tog. *(14 sts)*

Row 3: Knit.

Row 4: Purl.

Row 5: Inc, k2, inc, k1, inc, k2, inc, k1, inc, k2, inc. *(20 sts)*

Row 6: Purl.

Row 7: [Inc, k2] twice, inc, k6, [inc, k2] twice, inc. *(26 sts)*

Row 8: Purl.

Row 9: K18, wrap and turn.

Row 10: P10, w&t.

Row 11: K10, w&t.

Row 12: P10, w&t.

Row 13: K10, w&t.

Row 14: P10, w&t.

Row 15: K across all sts. *(26 sts)*

Row 16: Purl.

Row 17: K19, turn.

Next row: P12, turn.

Work top of head on center 12 sts.

Next row: K2tog, k8, k2tog. *(10 sts)*

Next row: Purl.

Next row: K2tog, k6, k2tog. *(8 sts)*

Next row: Purl.

Next row: K2tog, k4, k2tog. *(6 sts)*

Next row: [P2tog] 3 times. *(3 sts)*

Next row: K3tog and fasten off.

With RS facing, rejoin yarn to 7 sts on left of center 12 sts, k2tog, k5. *(6 sts)*

Next row: Purl.

Next row: K2tog, k2, k2tog. *(4 sts)*

Next row: [P2tog] twice. *(2 sts)*

Next row: K2tog and fasten off.

With WS facing, rejoin yarn to rem 7 sts, p2tog, p5. *(6 sts)*

Next row: Knit.

Next row: P2tog, p2, p2tog. *(4 sts)*

Next row: [K2tog] twice. *(2 sts)*

Next row: P2tog and fasten off.

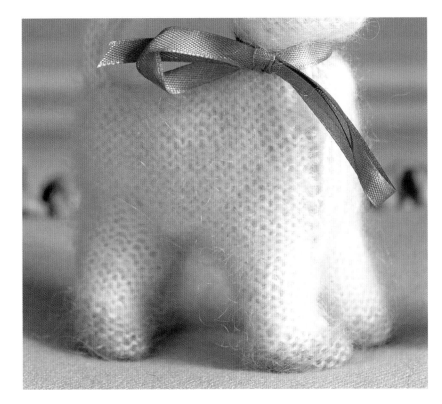

Coat
The kitten is sewn up with the wrong side of the knitting on the outside for extra fluffiness.

Head

We've used transparent nylon thread for the whiskers, which is realistic but has a tendency to fall out. Cream sewing thread also looks good, and stays in place better.

Tummy

With US 2 (2¾mm) needles and cr, cast on 2 sts.
Work 2 rows st st.
Row 3: [Inc] twice. *(4 sts)*
Work 11 rows st st.
Row 15: Inc, k2, inc. *(6 sts)*
Work 11 rows st st.
Row 27: K2tog, k2, k2tog. *(4 sts)*
Work 11 rows st st.
Row 39: Inc, k2, inc. *(6 sts)*
Work 15 rows st st.
Row 55: K2tog, k2, k2tog. *(4 sts)*
Row 56: [P2tog] twice. *(2 sts)*
Row 57: K2tog and fasten off.

Ear

(make 2 the same)
With US 2 (2¾mm) needles and cr, cast on 6 sts.
Work 4 rows garter st.
Row 5: K2tog, k2, k2tog. *(4 sts)*
Row 6: [K2tog] twice. *(2 sts)*
Row 7: K2tog and fasten off.

Tail

To make this kitten, turn the Left Side of Body and Right Side of Body so the wrong side (reverse st st) faces out. When finishing the kitten, this side will be used as the right side (see To Finish).
With US 2 (2¾mm) double-pointed needles and cr and chosen RS facing, k4 from spare needle of Right Side of Body for Tail, then k4 from spare needle of Left Side of Body for Tail. *(8 sts)*
Work in i-cord as follows:
Knit 12 rows.
Row 13: K2tog, k4, k2tog. *(6 sts)*
Knit 2 rows.
Row 16: K2tog, k2, k2tog. *(4 sts)*
Row 17: [K2tog] twice. *(2 sts)*
Row 18: K2tog and fasten off.

To Finish

This kitten is sewn up with the wrong side on the outside (as it's fluffier); the only parts that are the right side out are the tummy and tail. Sew in ends, leaving ends from bound off rows for sewing up. Using mattress or whip stitch, sew up legs starting at paw. Using mattress or whip stitch, sew along back of kitten and down bottom. Sew sides of cheeks together with whip stitch. Using mattress or whip stitch, sew cast on row of tummy to bottom end of kitten and sew final row to under chin. Ease and sew tummy to fit body, matching curves to legs. Leave a 1in (2.5cm) gap between front and back legs on one side. Roll the pipecleaners in a small amount of stuffing and bend each one into a U shape. Fold over the ends (so they don't poke out of the paws) and slip into body, one pipecleaner down front legs and one down back legs. Stuff, and sew up gap with mattress stitch. Mold into shape. Sew ears to head, leaving about 3 sts between the two ears. For the eyes, use sa yarn to make round French knots. Work each knot over 2 sts and wrap the yarn around the needle five times, push needle back through same hole, and sew down with a small stitch at bottom of knot to form a circle. For nose, use po yarn to embroider three parallel lines at point of nose, two long and one short. For whiskers, cut three 3in (8cm) strands of transparent nylon and thread through cheeks, then trim. Tie ribbon around neck if desired.

Tabby Kitten Sitting

This kitten is quick and easy to knit, and can sit in the palm of your hand.

Measurements

Length: 5¼in (13cm)
Height to top of head: 4½in (11cm)

Materials

- Pair of US 2 (2¾mm) knitting needles
- 2 spare US 2 (2¾mm) knitting needles or small stitch holders or safety pins
- Pair of US 2 (2¾mm) double-pointed knitting needles
- ⅛oz (5g) of Rowan Kidsilk Haze in Pearl 590 (pe)
- 1oz (20g) of Rowan Kidsilk Haze in Smoke 605 (sm)
- Tiny amount of Rowan Pure Wool 4ply in Powder 443 (po) for nose
- Tiny amount of Rowan Pure Wool 4ply in Sage 448 (sa) for eyes
- 2 pipecleaners
- White sewing thread for whiskers
- Ribbon for neck

Abbreviations

See page 141.
See page 141 for Wrap Method.

Back Leg

(make 2 the same)
With US 2 (2¾mm) needles and 2 ends of pe, cast on 13 sts.
Work 4 rows st st.
Add 1 end of sm (3 ends in total) and work 2 rows st st.
Row 7: [Inc] twice, k1, inc, k5, inc, k1, [inc] twice. *(19 sts)*
Row 8: [Inc] twice, p15, [inc] twice. *(23 sts)*
Row 9: [Inc] twice, k19, [inc] twice. *(27 sts)*
Work 3 rows st st.
Row 13: [K2tog] 3 times, k15, [k2tog] 3 times. *(21 sts)*
Row 14: [P2tog] 3 times, p9, [p2tog] 3 times. *(15 sts)*
Row 15: [K2tog] 3 times, k3, [k2tog] 3 times. *(9 sts)*
Row 16: [P2tog] twice, p1, [p2tog] twice. *(5 sts)*
Bind off 5 sts.

Right Front Leg

With US 2 (2¾mm) needles and 2 ends of pe, cast on 13 sts.
Beg with a k row, work 2 rows st st.
Row 3: K2tog, inc, k7, inc, k2tog. *(13 sts)*
Row 4: Purl.
Add 1 end of sm (3 ends in total) and rep last 2 rows once more.
Work 6 rows st st.
Row 13: Inc, k11, inc. *(15 sts)*
Row 14: Purl.*
Row 15: Bind off 8 sts, k to end (hold 7 sts on spare needle for Right Side of Body).

Left Front Leg

Work as for Right Front Leg to *.
Row 15: K7, bind off 8 sts (hold 7 sts on spare needle for Left Side of Body).

Right Side of Body

With US 2 (2¾mm) needles and 2 ends of sm and 1 of pe, cast on 4 sts.
Beg with a k row, work 2 rows st st.
Row 3: Inc, k3. *(5 sts)*
Row 4: P4, inc. *(6 sts)*
Row 5: Inc, k5. *(7 sts)*
Row 6: P6, inc. *(8 sts)*
Row 7: Inc, k7. *(9 sts)*
Row 8: P8, inc. *(10 sts)*
Row 9: Inc, k9. *(11 sts)*
Row 10: Purl.
Row 11: Inc, k10. *(12 sts)*
Row 12: Purl.
Row 13: Inc, k11. *(13 sts)*
Row 14: Purl.
Row 15: Inc, k12. *(14 sts)*
Row 16: P14, with WS facing p7 from spare needle of Right Front Leg. *(21 sts)*
Row 17: Inc, k18, k2tog. *(21 sts)*
Work 3 rows st st.
Row 21: K19, k2tog. *(20 sts)*
Row 22: Bind off 4 sts, p to end. *(16 sts)*
Row 23: K14, k2tog. *(15 sts)*
Row 24: P2tog, p13. *(14 sts)*
Row 25: K2tog, k10, k2tog. *(12 sts)*
Row 26: P2tog, p10. *(11 sts)*
Row 27: K2tog, k7, k2tog. *(9 sts)*
Row 28: P2tog, p7 (hold 8 sts on spare needle for Neck).

Left Side of Body

With US 2 (2¾mm) needles and 2 ends of sm and 1 of pe, cast on 4 sts.
Beg with a p row, work 2 rows st st.
Row 3: Inc, p3. *(5 sts)*
Row 4: K4, inc. *(6 sts)*
Row 5: Inc, p5. *(7 sts)*
Row 6: K6, inc. *(8 sts)*
Row 7: Inc, p7. *(9 sts)*
Row 8: K8, inc. *(10 sts)*
Row 9: Inc, p9. *(11 sts)*
Row 10: Knit.
Row 11: Inc, p10. *(12 sts)*
Row 12: Knit.
Row 13: Inc, p11. *(13 sts)*
Row 14: Knit.
Row 15: Inc, p12. *(14 sts)*
Row 16: K14, with RS facing k7 from spare needle of Left Front Leg. *(21 sts)*
Row 17: Inc, p18, p2tog. *(21 sts)*

Head

This kitten has a ribbon, but you can knit a collar if you prefer.

Work 3 rows st st.
Row 21: P19, p2tog. *(20 sts)*
Row 22: Bind off 4 sts, k to end. *(16 sts)*
Row 23: P14, p2tog. *(15 sts)*
Row 24: K2tog, k13. *(14 sts)*
Row 25: P2tog, p10, p2tog. *(12 sts)*
Row 26: K2tog, k10. *(11 sts)*
Row 27: P2tog, p7, p2tog. *(9 sts)*
Row 28: K2tog, k7 (hold 8 sts on spare needle for Neck).

Neck and Head

Row 1: With US 2 (2¾mm) needles and 2 ends of sm and 1 of pe and RS facing, k8 from spare needle of Right Side of Body, then k8 from spare needle of Left Side of Body. *(16 sts)*
Row 2: P2tog, p12, p2tog. *(14 sts)*
Row 3: Knit.
Row 4: Purl.
Row 5: Inc, k2, inc, k1, inc, k2, inc, k1, inc, k2, inc. *(20 sts)*
Row 6: Purl.
Row 7: K2, inc, k2, [inc] twice, k6, [inc] twice, k2, inc, k2. *(26 sts)*
Row 8: Purl.
Row 9: K18, wrap and turn.
Row 10: P10, w&t.
Row 11: K10, w&t.
Row 12: P10, w&t.
Row 13: K10, w&t.
Row 14: P10, w&t.
Row 15: K across all sts. *(26 sts)*
Row 16: Purl.
Row 17: K19, turn.
Next row: P12, turn.
Work top of head on center 12 sts.
Next row: K2tog, k8, k2tog. *(10 sts)*
Next row: Purl.
Next row: K2tog, k6, k2tog. *(8 sts)*
Next row: Purl.
Next row: K2tog, k4, k2tog. *(6 sts)*
Next row: [P2tog] 3 times. *(3 sts)*
Next row: K3tog, break off yarn.

With RS facing, rejoin yarn to 7 sts on left of center 12 sts, k2tog, k5. *(6 sts)*
Next row: Purl.
Next row: K2tog, k2, k2tog. *(4 sts)*
Next row: [P2tog] twice. *(2 sts)*
Next row: K2tog and fasten off.
With WS facing, rejoin yarn to rem 7 sts, p2tog, p5. *(6 sts)*
Next row: Knit.
Next row: P2tog, p2, p2tog. *(4 sts)*
Next row: [K2tog] twice. *(2 sts)*
Next row: P2tog and fasten off.

Tummy

With US 2 (2¾mm) needles and 2 ends of pe, cast on 5 sts.
Work 4 rows st st.
Row 5: Inc, k3, inc. *(7 sts)*
Row 6: Purl.
Work 30 rows st st.
Row 37: Inc, k5, inc. *(9 sts)*
Row 38: Purl.
Work 8 rows st st.
Row 47: K2tog, k5, k2tog. *(7 sts)*
Row 48: P2tog, p3, p2tog. *(5 sts)*
Row 49: K2tog, k1, k2tog. *(3 sts)*
Row 50: P3tog and fasten off.

Ear

(make 2 the same)
With US 2 (2¾mm) needles and 2 ends of pe and 1 of sm, cast on 6 sts.
Work 4 rows garter st.
Row 5: K2tog, k2, k2tog. *(4 sts)*
Row 6: [K2tog] twice. *(2 sts)*
Row 7: K2tog and fasten off.

Tail

With US 2 (2¾mm) double-pointed needles and 2 ends of sm and 1 of pe, cast on 8 sts.
Work in i-cord as follows:
Knit 12 rows.
Row 13: K2tog, k4, k2tog. *(6 sts)*
Knit 2 rows.

Row 16: K2tog, k2, k2tog. *(4 sts)*
Row 17: [K2tog] twice. *(2 sts)*
Row 18: K2tog and fasten off.

To Finish

This kitten is sewn up with the wrong side on the outside (as it's fluffier); the only parts that are the right side out are the tummy and tail. Sew in ends, leaving ends from bound off rows for sewing up. Using mattress or whip stitch, sew up legs starting at paw. Cut a pipecleaner to fit length of back leg, fold over the ends (so they don't poke out of the paws), and slip into leg. Lightly stuff and sew along top of back legs, then bend into shape as shown in photograph. Using mattress or whip stitch, sew along back of kitten. Sew sides of cheeks together with whip stitch. Using mattress or whip stitch, sew cast on row of tummy to bottom end of kitten and sew final row to chin. Ease and sew tummy to fit body, matching curves to legs. Leave a 1in (2.5cm) gap on one side. Roll a pipecleaner in a small amount of stuffing and bend into a U shape. Fold over the ends (so they don't poke out of the paws) and slip into body down front legs. Stuff, and sew up gap with mattress stitch. Using whip stitch, attach back legs to body, then sew along top of leg and down back edge. To hold the legs in place, at about ½in (1cm) down from top of leg, sew the inside of the leg to the body. Mold into shape. Sew ears to head, leaving about 3 sts between the two ears. For the eyes, use sa yarn to make round French knots. Work each knot over 2 sts and wrap the yarn around the needle five times, push needle back through same hole, and sew down with a small stitch at bottom of knot to form a circle. For nose, use po yarn to embroider three parallel lines at point of nose, two long and one short. For whiskers, cut 2in (5cm) strands of sewing thread and thread through cheeks, then trim. Tie ribbon around neck.

Coat
Using a combination of colors of mohair yarn knitted together, you can easily get a variegated tabby look.

British Shorthair

Originating in Roman times, the Brit, as it's commonly known, is a cuddly toy cat—it is cuddly and placid, and looks a little like an animated toy. With its thick and luxurious fur, the British Shorthair is also one of the most enjoyable cats to stroke. The British Shorthair is reputed to be the model for the Cheshire Cat in *Alice's Adventures in Wonderland*, and these cats are the stars of numerous ads—Whiskas, Sheba, and, inexplicably, Bacardi Breezer. Mrs. McClusky's cat in *Desperate Housewives* is a British Shorthair.

British Shorthair

The British Shorthair is a rounded, well-stuffed cat that is easy to knit.

Measurements

Length: 6¼in (16cm)
Height to top of head: 5¼in (13cm)

Materials

- Pair of US 2 (2¾mm) knitting needles
- 4 spare US 2 (2¾mm) knitting needles or small stitch holders or safety pins
- Pair of US 2 (2¾mm) double-pointed knitting needles
- 1oz (20g) of Rowan Cashsoft 4ply in Thunder 437 (th)
- ¼oz (10g) of Rowan Kidsilk Haze in Anthracite 639 (an) used DOUBLE throughout
- Tiny amount of Rowan Pure Wool 4ply in Black 404 (bl) for nose
- Tiny amount of Rowan Cashsoft 4ply in Almond 458 (al) for eyes
- 2 pipecleaners
- Rice or lentils for stuffing
- Transparent nylon thread for whiskers

Abbreviations

See page 141.
See page 141 for Wrap Method.

Right Back Leg

With US 2 (2¾mm) needles and th and DOUBLE an held together, cast on 11 sts. Beg with a k row, work 4 rows st st.
Row 5: Inc, k2, k2tog, k1, k2tog, k2, inc. *(11 sts)*
Row 6: Purl.
Rep last 2 rows three times more.
Row 13: K2tog, k2, inc, k1, inc, k2, k2tog. *(11 sts)*
Row 14: Purl.
Rep last 2 rows once more.
Row 17: Inc, k9, inc. *(13 sts)*
Row 18: Purl.
Row 19: Inc, k11, inc. *(15 sts)*
Row 20: Purl.*
Row 21: Bind off 7 sts, k to end (hold 8 sts on spare needle for Right Side of Body).

Left Back Leg

Work as for Right Back Leg to *.
Row 21: K8, bind off 7 sts (hold 8 sts on spare needle for Left Side of Body).

Right Front Leg

With US 2 (2¾mm) needles and th and DOUBLE an held together, cast on 11 sts. Beg with a k row, work 6 rows st st.
Row 7: K2tog, k7, k2tog. *(9 sts)*
Row 8: Purl.
Work 2 rows st st.
Row 11: Inc, k7, inc. *(11 sts)*
Row 12: Purl.
Row 13: Inc, k9, inc. *(13 sts)*
Work 3 rows st st. **
Row 17: Bind off 6 sts (hold 7 sts on spare needle for Right Side of Body).

Left Front Leg

Work as for Right Front Leg to **.
Row 17: K7, bind off 6 sts (hold 7 sts on spare needle for Left Side of Body).

Right Side of Body

Row 1: With US 2 (2¾mm) needles and th and DOUBLE an held together, cast on 2 sts, with RS facing k7 from spare needle of Right Front Leg, cast on 12 sts, k8 from spare needle of Right Back Leg, cast on 2 sts. *(31 sts)*
Work 3 rows st st.
Row 5: Inc, k30. *(32 sts)*
Work 3 rows st st.
Row 9: Inc, k31. *(33 sts)*
Work 3 rows st st.
Row 13: Inc, k32. *(34 sts)*
Work 4 rows st st.
Row 18: P4 (hold these 4 sts on spare needle for Tail), p30. *(30 sts)*
Row 19: K9 (hold these 9 sts on spare needle for Neck), bind off 21 sts.

Left Side of Body

Row 1: With US 2 (2¾mm) needles and th and DOUBLE an held together, cast on 2 sts, with WS facing p7 from spare needle of Left Front Leg, cast on 12 sts, p8 from spare needle of Left Back Leg, cast on 2 sts. *(31 sts)*
Work 3 rows st st.
Row 5: Inc, p30. *(32 sts)*
Work 3 rows st st.
Row 9: Inc, p31. *(33 sts)*
Work 3 rows st st.
Row 13: Inc, p32. *(34 sts)*
Work 4 rows st st.
Row 18: K4 (hold these 4 sts on spare needle for Tail), k30. *(30 sts)*
Row 19: P9 (hold these 9 sts on spare needle for Neck), bind off 21 sts.

Neck and Head

Row 1: With US 2 (2¾mm) needles and th and DOUBLE an held together and RS facing, k9 from spare needle of Right Side of Body for Neck, then k9 from spare needle of Left Side of Body for Neck. *(18 sts)*
Row 2: Inc, p16, inc. *(20 sts)*

Row 3: K16, wrap and turn.
Row 4: P12, w&t.
Row 5: K12, w&t.
Row 6: P12, w&t.
Row 7: Knit to end. *(20 sts in total)*
Row 8: Purl.
Row 9: Inc, k18, inc. *(22 sts)*
Row 10: Purl.
Row 11: Inc, k20, inc. *(24 sts)*
Row 12: Purl.
Row 13: K17, wrap and turn.
Row 14: P10, w&t.
Row 15: K10, w&t.
Row 16: P10, w&t.
Row 17: K to end. *(24 sts in total)*
Row 18: P3, [p2tog] 9 times, p3. *(15 sts)*
Row 19: K1, [k2tog] 3 times, k1, [k2tog] 3 times, k1. *(9 sts)*
Row 20: [P3tog] 3 times. *(3 sts)*
Row 21: K3tog and fasten off.

Tummy

With US 2 (2¾mm) needles and th and DOUBLE an held together, cast on 2 sts.
Beg with a k row, work 4 rows st st.
Row 5: [Inc] twice. *(4 sts)*
Work 3 rows st st.
Row 9: Inc, k2, inc. *(6 sts)*
Work 15 rows st st.
Row 25: K2tog, k2, k2tog. *(4 sts)*
Work 9 rows st st.
Row 35: Inc, k2, inc. *(6 sts)*
Work 21 rows st st.
Row 57: K2tog, k2, k2tog. *(4 sts)*
Work 5 rows st st.
Row 63: [K2tog] twice. *(2 sts)*
Row 64: P2tog and fasten off.

Ear

(make 2 the same)
With US 2 (2¾mm) needles and th and DOUBLE an held together, cast on 6 sts.
Beg with a k row, work 4 rows st st.
Row 5: K2tog, k2, k2tog. *(4 sts)*

Row 6: Purl.
Row 7: [K2tog] twice. *(2 sts)*
Row 8: P2tog and fasten off.

Tail

With US 2 (2¾mm) double-pointed needles and th and DOUBLE an held together and RS facing, k4 from spare needle of Left Side of Body for Tail, then k4 from spare needle of Right Side of Body for Tail. *(8 sts)*
Work in i-cord as follows:
Knit 8 rows.
Row 9: K2tog, k4, k2tog. *(6 sts)*
Knit 11 rows.
Row 21: K2tog, k2, k2tog. *(4 sts)*
Knit 2 rows.
Row 24: [K2tog] twice. *(2 sts)*
Row 25: K2tog and fasten off.

Tail

To convey the richness of his coat, we have knitted our British Shorthair in a mixture of 4ply and mohair yarns. We have also put a pipecleaner in his tail so that you can manipulate it, but this is far from vital.

To Finish

Sew in ends, leaving ends from bound off rows for sewing up. Using mattress or whip stitch, sew up legs starting at paw. Using mattress or whip stitch, sew along back of cat and down bottom. Using mattress or whip stitch, sew cast on row of tummy to bottom end of cat and sew final row to nose. Ease and sew tummy to fit body, matching curves to legs. Leave a 1in (2.5cm) gap between front and back legs on one side. Roll the pipecleaners in a small amount of stuffing and bend each one into a U shape. Fold over the ends (so they don't poke out of the paws) and slip into body, one pipecleaner down front legs and one down back legs. Stuff, adding rice or lentils in tummy if you want to add characteristic weight, and sew up gap with mattress stitch. Mold into shape. Sew ears to head as in photograph. For the eyes, use al yarn to make elongated French knots. Work each knot over 2 sts at an angle and wrap the yarn around the needle five times. With th yarn, make a stitch over the center of the French knot. For nose, use bl yarn to embroider three parallel lines at point of nose, two long and one short. For whiskers, cut 4in (10cm) strands of transparent nylon and thread through cheeks, then trim.

British Shorthair Curled Up

The British Shorthair has particularly chubby cheeks—think Cheshire Cat for shape. When you knit the wrap & turn sections on the body of this cat, you move in one stitch at the beginning of each row, as described in the pattern.

Measurements
Length: 4½in (11cm)

Materials
- Pair of US 2 (2¾mm) knitting needles
- Pair of US 2 (2¾mm) double-pointed knitting needles
- 1oz (20g) of Rowan Cashsoft 4ply in Thunder 437 (th)
- ¼oz (10g) of Rowan Kidsilk Haze in Anthracite 639 (an) used DOUBLE throughout
- Tiny amount of Rowan Pure Wool 4ply in Black 404 (bl) for nose and eyes
- Transparent nylon thread for whiskers
- Rice or lentils for stuffing
- 1 pipecleaner

Abbreviations
See page 141.
See page 141 for Wrap Method.

Back Leg
With US 2 (2¾mm) needles and th and DOUBLE an held together, cast on 7 sts.
Beg with a k row, work 12 rows st st.
Row 13: Inc, k1, inc, k1, inc, k1, inc. *(11 sts)*
Row 14: Purl.
Row 15: K4, inc, k1, inc, k4. *(13 sts)*
Row 16: Purl.
Row 17: K5, inc, k1, inc, k5. *(15 sts)*
Row 18: Purl.
Row 19: K6, inc, k1, inc, k6. *(17 sts)*
Row 20: Purl.
Row 21: K7, inc, k1, inc, k7. *(19 sts)*
Work 5 rows st st.
Row 27: K7, k2tog, k1, k2tog, k7. *(17 sts)*
Row 28: P6, p2tog, p1, p2tog, p6. *(15 sts)*
Row 29: K5, k2tog, k1, k2tog, k5. *(13 sts)*
Row 30: Purl.
Bind off.

Body and Head
(knitted in one piece)
With US 2 (2¾mm) needles and th and DOUBLE an held together, cast on 20 sts.
Row 1: Knit.
Row 2: Purl.
Row 3: K8, inc, k2, inc, k8. *(22 sts)*
Row 4: Purl.
Row 5: K9, inc, k2, inc, k9. *(24 sts)*
Row 6: Purl.
Row 7: K10, inc, k2, inc, k10. *(26 sts)*
Row 8: Purl.
Row 9: K24, wrap and turn.
Row 10: P22, w&t.
Row 11: K9, inc, k2, inc, k8, w&t. *(23 sts)*
Row 12: P22, w&t. *(22 sts)*
Row 13: K21, w&t. *(21 sts)*
Row 14: P20, w&t. *(20 sts)*
Row 15: K8, inc, k2, inc, k7, w&t. *(21 sts)*
Row 16: P20, w&t. *(20 sts)*
Row 17: K19, w&t. *(19 sts)*
Row 18: P18, w&t. *(18 sts)*
Row 19: Knit to end. *(30 sts on right-hand needle)*

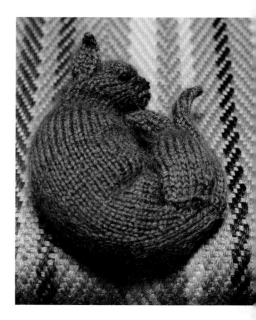

Back
His tail is sewn to his leg and his leg is sewn to his chin to make his back curl properly. He has one horizontal stitch for a closed eye.

Row 20: Purl.
Row 21: K13, inc, k2, inc, k13. *(32 sts)*
Row 22: Purl.
Row 23: Inc, k30, inc. *(34 sts)*
Row 24: Purl.
Row 25: K32, wrap and turn.
Row 26: P30, w&t. *(30 sts)*
Row 27: K13, inc, k2, inc, k12, w&t. *(31 sts)*
Row 28: P30, w&t. *(30 sts)*
Row 29: K29, w&t. *(29 sts)*
Row 30: P28, w&t. *(28 sts)*
Row 31: K27, w&t. *(27 sts)*
Row 32: P26, w&t. *(26 sts)*
Row 33: K10, inc, k2, inc, k17. *(38 sts on right-hand needle)*
Row 34: Purl.
Row 35: Knit.
Row 36: Purl.
Row 37: K35, wrap and turn.
Row 38: P32, w&t.
Row 39: K31, w&t. *(31 sts)*
Row 40: P30, w&t. *(30 sts)*
Row 41: K12, k2tog, k2, k2tog, k12, w&t. *(28 sts)*
Row 42: P26, w&t. *(26 sts)*
Row 43: K9, k2tog, k2, k2tog, k9, w&t. *(22 sts)*
Row 44: P22, w&t.
Row 45: Knit to end. *(34 sts on right-hand needle)*
Row 46: Purl.
Row 47: K2tog, k10, k2tog, k6, k2tog, k10, k2tog. *(30 sts)*
Row 48: Purl.
Row 49: K2tog, k8, k2tog, k6, k2tog, k8, k2tog. *(26 sts)*
Row 50: P2tog, p6, p2tog, p6, p2tog, p6, p2tog. *(22 sts)*
Row 51: K2tog, k5, k2tog, k4, k2tog, k5, k2tog. *(18 sts)*
Row 52: Purl.
Row 53: Knit.
Row 54: P7, inc, p2, inc, p7. *(20 sts)*
Row 55: K16, wrap and turn.

Row 56: P12, w&t.
Row 57: K12, w&t.
Row 58: P12, w&t.
Row 59: K12, w&t.
Row 60: P12, w&t.
Row 61: K to end. *(20 sts on right-hand needle)*
Row 62: Inc, p18, inc. *(22 sts)*
Row 63: Inc, k20, inc. *(24 sts)*
Row 64: Purl.
Row 65: K17, wrap and turn.
Row 66: P10, w&t.
Row 67: K10, w&t.
Row 68: P10, w&t.
Row 69: Knit to end. *(24 sts)*
Row 70: P3, [p2tog] 9 times, p3. *(15 sts)*
Row 71: K1, [k2tog] 3 times, k1, [k2tog] 3 times, k1. *(9 sts)*
Row 72: [P3tog] 3 times. *(3 sts)*
Row 73: K3tog and fasten off.

Ear
(make 2 the same)
With US 2 (2¾mm) needles and th and DOUBLE an held together, cast on 6 sts.
Work 4 rows st st.
Row 5: K2tog, k2, k2tog. *(4 sts)*
Row 6: Purl.
Row 7: [K2tog] twice. *(2 sts)*
Row 8: P2tog and fasten off.

Tail
With US 2 (2¾mm) double-pointed needles and th and DOUBLE an held together, cast on 6 sts.
Work in i-cord as follows:
Knit 23 rows.
Row 24: K2tog, k2, k2tog. *(4 sts)*
Knit 2 rows.
Row 27: [K2tog] twice. *(2 sts)*
Row 28: K2tog and fasten off.

To Finish
Sew in ends, leaving ends from bound off rows for sewing up. Using mattress or whip stitch, sew up leg starting at paw. Using mattress or whip stitch, sew along tummy and head, leaving a 1in (2.5cm) gap. Cut a pipecleaner to just longer than cat, fold over the ends, and slip into body and head. The pipecleaner is useful for adding to the curved back and head position. Stuff with rice or lentils to give the sleeping cat more weight, and sew up gap with mattress stitch. Mold into shape. Attach leg and tail as in photograph. With a little stitch, attach the paw and the tip of tail to body. Sew ears to head, leaving about 3 sts between the two ears. For the eyes, use bl yarn to make one stitch. Using bl yarn, embroider a small nose in satin stitch. For whiskers, cut 3in (8cm) strands of transparent nylon and thread through cheeks, then trim.

Devon Rex

The freerunner of the feline world, Devon Rex cats are agile, prone to showing off, and keen on heights—they are able to climb up walls and drapes effortlessly. The Devon Rex is a highly unusual looking creature, sometimes described as a 'monkey in a cat suit' and also known as the pixie or alien cat. Devon Rex also wag their tails when happy, which has led to them being called poodle cats.

Devon Rex

The Devon Rex is knitted in boucle yarn to give the impression of the characteristic short curly coat.

Measurements

Length: 6in (15cm)
Height to top of ears: 5¼in (13cm)

Materials

- Pair of US 2 (2¾mm) knitting needles
- 2 spare US 2 (2¾mm) knitting needles or small stitch holders or safety pins
- Pair of US 2 (2¾mm) double-pointed knitting needles
- 1½oz (30g) of Halcyon Yarn Gemstone Silk Bouclé in Taupe 104 (ta)
- Small amount of Rowan Cashsoft 4ply in Cream 433 (cr)
- Tiny amount of Rowan Cashsoft 4ply in Almond 458 (al) for eyes
- Tiny amount of Rowan Pure Wool 4ply in Black 404 (bl) for pupils
- 2 pipecleaners
- Transparent nylon thread for whiskers

Abbreviations

See page 141.
See page 141 for Wrap Method.

Back Leg

(make 2 the same)
With US 2 (2¾mm) needles and ta, cast on 7 sts.
Beg with a k row, work 10 rows st st.
Row 11: K1, inc into next 5 sts, k1. *(12 sts)*
Row 12: Purl.
Row 13: K1, inc into next 3 sts, k4, inc into next 3 sts, k1. *(18 sts)*
Work 9 rows st st.
Row 23: K2tog, k14, k2tog. *(16 sts)*
Row 24: Purl.
Row 25: K2tog, k12, k2tog. *(14 sts)*
Row 26: Purl.
Row 27: K2tog, k10, k2tog. *(12 sts)*
Row 28: P2tog, p8, p2tog. *(10 sts)*
Row 29: K2tog, k6, k2tog. *(8 sts)*
Row 30: Purl.
Bind off.

Right Front Leg

With US 2 (2¾mm) needles and ta, cast on 7 sts.
Beg with a k row, work 12 rows st st.
Row 13: Inc, k5, inc. *(9 sts)*
Row 14: Purl.
Row 15: Inc, k7, inc. *(11 sts)*
Row 16: Purl.
Row 17: Knit.
Row 18: Purl.*
Row 19: Bind off 5 sts, k to end (hold 6 sts on spare needle for Right Side of Body).

Left Front Leg

Work as for Right Front Leg to *.
Row 19: K6, bind off 5 sts (hold 6 sts on spare needle for Left Side of Body).

Right Side of Body

With US 2 (2¾mm) needles and ta, cast on 5 sts.
Beg with a k row, work 2 rows st st.
Row 3: Inc, k4. *(6 sts)*
Row 4 and foll 7 alt rows: Purl.
Row 5: Inc, k5. *(7 sts)*
Row 7: Inc, k6. *(8 sts)*
Row 9: Inc, k7. *(9 sts)*
Row 11: Inc, k8. *(10 sts)*
Row 13: Inc, k9. *(11 sts)*
Row 15: Inc, k10. *(12 sts)*
Row 17: Inc, k11. *(13 sts)*
Row 19: Inc, k12, *(14 sts)*
Row 20: P14, with WS facing p6 from spare needle of Right Front Leg, cast on 1 st. *(21 sts)*
Work 5 rows st st.
Row 26: P2tog, p19. *(20 sts)*
Row 27: K18, k2tog. *(19 sts)*
Row 28: P2tog, p17. *(18 sts)*
Row 29: Inc, k17. *(19 sts)*
Row 30: Bind off 5 sts, p to end. *(14 sts)*
Row 31: K12, k2tog. *(13 sts)*
Row 32: P2tog, p11. *(12 sts)*
Row 33: K2tog, k8, k2tog. *(10 sts)*
Row 34: P2tog, p8. *(9 sts)*
Row 35: K2tog, k5, k2tog. *(7 sts)*
Row 36: P2tog, p5. *(6 sts)*
Row 37: K2tog, k2, k2tog. *(4 sts)*
Work 3 rows st st (hold 4 sts on spare needle for Neck).

Left Side of Body

With US 2 (2¾mm) needles and ta, cast on 5 sts.
Beg with a p row, work 2 rows st st.
Row 3: Inc, p4. *(6 sts)*
Row 4 and foll 7 alt rows: Knit.
Row 5: Inc, p5. *(7 sts)*
Row 7: Inc, p6, *(8 sts)*
Row 9: Inc, p7. *(9 sts)*
Row 11: Inc, p8. *(10 sts)*
Row 13: Inc, p9. *(11 sts)*
Row 15: Inc, p10. *(12 sts)*
Row 17: Inc, p11. *(13 sts)*
Row 19: Inc, p12, *(14 sts)*
Row 20: K14, with RS facing k6 from spare needle of Left Front Leg, cast on 1 st. *(21 sts)*
Work 5 rows st st.

Back
To maintain his delicate silhouette,
don't overstuff the Devon Rex.

Ears

Devon Rex cats have enormous ears, which are slightly pinched before sewing on to prevent curling (see page 140).

Row 26: K2tog, k19. *(20 sts)*
Row 27: P18, p2tog. *(19 sts)*
Row 28: K2tog, k17. *(18 sts)*
Row 29: Inc, p17. *(19 sts)*
Row 30: Bind off 5 sts, k to end. *(14 sts)*
Row 31: P12, p2tog. *(13 sts)*
Row 32: K2tog, k11. *(12 sts)*
Row 33: P2tog, p8, p2tog. *(10 sts)*
Row 34: K2tog, k8. *(9 sts)*
Row 35: P2tog, p5, p2tog. *(7 sts)*
Row 36: K2tog, k5. *(6 sts)*
Row 37: P2tog, p2, p2tog. *(4 sts)*
Work 3 rows st st (hold 4 sts on spare needle for Neck).

Neck and Head

Row 1: With US 2 (2¾mm) and ta and RS facing, k4 from spare needle of Right Side of Body, then k4 from spare needle of Left Side of Body. *(8 sts)*
Work 3 rows st st.
Row 5: Inc, k1, inc, k2, inc, k1, inc. *(12 sts)*
Row 6: Inc, p1, inc, p6, inc, p1, inc. *(16 sts)*
Row 7: K13, wrap and turn.
Row 8: P10, w&t.
Row 9: K10, w&t.
Row 10: P10, w&t.
Row 11: Knit to end. *(16 sts on right-hand needle)*
Row 12: Purl.
Row 13: K13, wrap and turn.
Row 14: P10, w&t.
Row 15: K10, w&t.
Row 16: P10, w&t.
Row 17: Knit to end. *(16 sts on right-hand needle)*
Row 18: [P2tog] 3 times, p4, [p2tog] 3 times. *(10 sts)*
Row 19: [K2tog] twice, k2, [k2tog] twice. *(6 sts)*
Row 20: P2tog, p2, p2tog. *(4 sts)*
Row 21: [K2tog] twice. *(2 sts)*
Row 22: P2tog and fasten off.

Tummy

With US 2 (2¾mm) and ta, cast on 2 sts.
Beg with a k row, work 2 rows st st.
Row 3: [Inc] twice. *(4 sts)*
Row 4: Purl.
Row 5: Inc, k2, inc. *(6 sts)*
Work 13 rows st st.
Join in cr.
Row 19: K2ta, k2cr, k2ta.
Row 20: P1ta, p4cr, p1ta.
Cont in cr.
Work 14 rows st st.
Row 35: Inc, k4, inc. *(8 sts)*
Row 36: Purl.
Row 37: Inc, k6, inc. *(10 sts)*
Row 38: Purl.
Row 39: K2tog, k6, k2tog. *(8 sts)*
Row 40: P2tog, p4, p2tog. *(6 sts)*
Row 41: K2tog, k2, k2tog. *(4 sts)*
Row 42: [P2tog] twice. *(2 sts)*
Row 43: K2tog and fasten off.

Ear

(make 2 the same)
With US 2 (2¾mm) needles and ta, cast on
7 sts.
Beg with a k row, work 6 rows st st.
Row 7: K2tog, k3, k2tog. *(5 sts)*
Row 8: Purl.
Row 9: K2tog, k2, k2tog. *(3 sts)*
Row 10: Purl.
Row 11: K2tog, k1. *(2 sts)*
Row 12: P2tog and fasten off.

Tail

With US 2 (2¾mm) double-pointed needles
and ta, cast on 4 sts.
Work in i-cord as follows:
Knit 8 rows.
Row 9: K2tog, k1. *(3 sts)*
Knit 12 rows.
Row 22: K2tog, k1. *(2 sts)*
Knit 6 rows.
Row 29: K2tog and fasten off.

To Finish

Sew in ends, leaving ends from bound off
rows for sewing up. Using mattress or whip
stitch, sew up front legs starting at paw.
Using mattress or whip stitch, sew along
back of cat and down bottom. Using
mattress or whip stitch, sew cast on row of
tummy to bottom end of cat and sew final
row to nose. Ease and sew tummy to fit
body. Leave a 1in (2.5cm) gap on one side.
Roll a pipecleaner in a small amount
stuffing and bend into a U shape. Fold over
the ends (so they don't poke out of the paws)
and slip into front legs. Stuff, and sew up
gap with mattress stitch. Cut a pipecleaner
to fit length of back leg, fold over the ends
(so they don't poke out of the paws), and slip
into leg. Lightly stuff and sew along top of
back legs, then bend into shape as shown in
photograph. Using whip stitch and with
seams at back, attach back legs to body,
sewing along top of leg and down back edge
as shown in photograph. To hold the legs in
place, at about ½in (1cm) down from top of
leg, sew through the leg, body, and opposite
leg on inside. Mold into shape. Attach the
tail, which can be positioned curled up or to
the side. Sew ears to head, pinching slightly
to prevent curling. For the eyes, use al yarn
to make round French knots. Work each
knot over 2 sts and wrap the yarn around
the needle five times, push needle back
through same hole, and sew down with a
small stitch at bottom of knot to form a
circle. With bl yarn, make a stitch in the
center of the French knot. For whiskers, cut
3in (8cm) strands of transparent nylon and
thread through cheeks, then trim.

Exotic

Abyssinian

Similar to the ancient Egyptian cats seen in paintings dating back over 3,000 years, the Abyssinian comes from Africa, but the exact country is uncertain. Although almost silent, these graceful and elegant cats love to explore, perhaps hearing a faint echo of their intrepid origins. They are also known as the Border Collie of the cat world, due to their boundless energy and curiosity. We used to have a beautiful Abyssinian called Cinto, who sucked earlobes.

Abyssinian

This is a refined cat that is also easy to knit.

Measurements

Length: 7in (18cm)
Height to top of head: 5¼in (13cm)

Materials

- Pair of US 2 (2¾mm) knitting needles
- 4 spare US 2 (2¾mm) knitting needles or small stitch holders or safety pins
- Pair of US 2 (2¾mm) double-pointed knitting needles
- ½oz (15g) of Rowan Felted Tweed in Cinnamon 175 (cn)
- ⅛oz (5g) of Rowan Pure Wool 4ply in Porcelaine 451 (pr)
- Tiny amount of Rowan Cashsoft 4ply in Bark 432 (bk)
- Tiny amount of Rowan Cashsoft 4ply in Kiwi 443 (ki) for eyes
- Tiny amount of Rowan Pure Wool 4ply in Black 404 (bl) for pupils
- 2 pipecleaners
- Crochet hook
- Cream sewing thread for whiskers

Abbreviations

See page 141.
See page 141 for Wrap Method.
See page 141 for Stranding or Fair Isle Technique.

Right Back Leg

With US 2 (2¾mm) needles and cn, cast on 7 sts.
Beg with a k row, work 2 rows st st.
Row 3: Inc, k2tog, k1, k2tog, inc. *(7 sts)*
Row 4: Purl.
Rep last 2 rows once more.
Work 5 rows st st.
Row 12: Inc, p5, inc. *(9 sts)*
Row 13: K2tog, inc into next 2 sts, k1, inc into next 2 sts, k2tog. *(11 sts)*
Row 14: P4, inc, p1, inc, p4. *(13 sts)*
Row 15: K5, inc, k1, inc, k5. *(15 sts)*
Row 16: Purl.
Row 17: K6, inc, k1, inc, k6. *(17 sts)*
Row 18: Purl.
Row 19: K7, inc, k1, inc, k7. *(19 sts)*
Row 20: Purl.
Row 21: K2tog, k6, inc, k1, inc, k6, k2tog. *(19 sts)*
Row 22: Purl.*
Row 23: Bind off 10 sts, k to end (hold 9 sts on spare needle for Right Side of Body).

Left Back Leg

Work as for Right Back Leg to *.
Row 23: K9, bind off 10 sts (hold 9 sts on spare needle for Left Side of Body).

Right Front Leg

With US 2 (2¾mm) needles and cn, cast on 7 sts.
Beg with a k row, work 2 rows st st.
Row 3: Inc, k2tog, k1, k2tog, inc. *(7 sts)*
Row 4: Purl.
Rep last 2 rows once more.
Work 6 rows st st.
Row 13: Inc, k5, inc. *(9 sts)*
Row 14: Purl.
Row 15: K2tog, k1, inc, k1, inc, k1, k2tog. *(9 sts)*
Row 16: Purl.
Row 17: K2tog, k1, inc, k1, inc, k1, k2tog. *(9 sts)*

Row 18: Purl.**
Row 19: Bind off 4 sts, k to end (hold 5 sts on spare needle for Right Side of Body).

Left Front Leg

Work as for Right Front Leg to **.
Row 19: K5, bind off 4 sts (hold 5 sts on spare needle for Left Side of Body).

Right Side of Body

Row 1: With US 2 (2¾mm) needles and cn, cast on 1 st, with RS facing k5 from spare needle of Right Front Leg, cast on 6 sts. *(12 sts)*
Row 2: Purl.
Row 3: K12, cast on 6 sts. *(18 sts)*
Row 4: Purl.
Row 5: Inc, k17, k9 from spare needle of Right Back Leg, cast on 1 st. *(29 sts)*
Work 2 rows st st.
Row 8: P28, inc. *(30 sts)*
Row 9: Inc, k29. *(31 sts)*
Row 10: P30, inc. *(32 sts)*
Work 3 rows st st.
Row 14: P2tog, p28, p2tog. *(30 sts)*
Row 15: K28, k2tog. *(29 sts)*
Row 16: Bind off 19 sts, p to end (hold 10 sts on spare needle for Neck).

Left Side of Body

Row 1: With US 2 (2¾mm) needles and cn, cast on 1 st, with WS facing p5 from spare needle of Left Front Leg, cast on 6 sts. *(12 sts)*
Row 2: Knit.
Row 3: P12, cast on 6 sts. *(18 sts)*
Row 4: Knit.
Row 5: Inc, p17, p9 from spare needle of Left Back Leg, cast on 1 st. *(29 sts)*
Work 2 rows st st.
Row 8: K28, inc. *(30 sts)*
Row 9: Inc, p29. *(31 sts)*
Row 10: K30, inc. *(32 sts)*
Work 3 rows st st.

Row 14: K2tog, k28, k2tog. *(30 sts)*
Row 15: P28, p2tog. *(29 sts)*
Row 16: Bind off 19 sts, k to end (hold 10 sts on spare needle for Neck).

Neck and Head

Row 1: With US 2 (2¾mm) needles and cn and RS facing, k2tog, k8 from spare needle of Right Side of Body, then k8, k2tog from spare needle of Left Side of Body. *(18 sts)*
Row 2: P6, p2tog, p2, p2tog, p6. *(16 sts)*
Row 3: K2tog, k12, k2tog. *(14 sts)*
Row 4: P4, p2tog, p2, p2tog, p4. *(12 sts)*
Row 5: Knit.
Row 6: P2tog, p8, p2tog. *(10 sts)*
Row 7: Inc, k8, inc. *(12 sts)*
Row 8: Inc, p10, inc. *(14 sts)*
Row 9: K12, wrap and turn.
Row 10: P10, w&t.
Row 11: K10, w&t.
Rep last 2 rows once more.
Row 14: P10, w&t.
Row 15: K12. *(14 sts in total)*
Row 16: Purl.
Row 17: K12, wrap and turn.
Join in bk.
Row 18: P4cn, p2bk, k4cn, w&t.
Row 19: K3cn, k4bk, k3cn, w&t.
Row 20: P2cn, p1bk, p4cn, p1bk, p2cn, w&t.
Row 21: K2cn, k1bk, k1cn, k2bk, k1cn, k1bk, k2cn, w&t.
Row 22: P2bk, p2cn, p2bk, p2cn, p1bk, p1cn, w&t.
Cont in cn.
Row 23: K12. *(14 sts in total)*
Row 24: P2tog, p1, [p2tog] 4 times, p1, p2tog. *(8 sts)*
Row 25: K1, k2tog, k2, k2tog, k1. *(6 sts)*
Row 26: Purl.
Row 27: K2tog, k2, k2tog. *(4 sts)*
Bind off.

Tummy

With US 2 (2¾mm) needles and pr, cast on 5 sts.
Beg with a k row, work 2 rows st st.
Row 3: K2tog, k1, k2tog. *(3 sts)*
Work 11 rows st st.
Row 15: Inc, k1, inc. *(5 sts)*
Work 21 rows st st.
Row 37: K2tog, k1, k2tog. *(3 sts)*
Work 5 rows st st.
Row 43: Inc, k1, inc. *(5 sts)*
Work 31 rows st st.
Row 75: K2tog, k1, k2tog. *(3 sts)*
Work 4 rows st st.
Row 80: P3tog and fasten off.

Head

When stuffing, make sure the neck is not overstuffed otherwise the cat will lose its graceful shape.

Tail

With US 2 (2¾mm) double-pointed needles
and cn, cast on 7 sts.
Work in i-cord as follows:
Knit 10 rows.
Row 11: K2tog, k3, k2tog. *(5 sts)*
Knit 16 rows.
Row 28: K2tog, k1, k2tog. *(3 sts)*
Row 29: K3tog and fasten off.

To Finish

Sew in ends, leaving ends from bound off
rows for sewing up. Using mattress or whip
stitch, sew up legs starting at paw. Using
mattress or whip stitch, sew along back of
cat and down bottom. At head, fold in half
and sew bound off edges of nose together.
Using mattress or whip stitch, sew cast on
row of tummy to bottom end of cat and sew
final row to nose. Ease and sew tummy to
fit body, matching curves to legs. Leave a
1in (2.5cm) gap between front and back legs
on one side. Roll the pipecleaners in a small
amount of stuffing and bend each one into
a U shape. Fold over the ends (so they don't
poke out of the paws) and slip into body,
one pipecleaner down front legs and one
down back legs. Stuff, and sew up gap with
mattress stitch. Mold into shape. Attach
the tail as in photograph. Sew ears to head,
leaving about 3 sts between the two ears.
Using a crochet hook and 2 strands of
unplied pr yarn, on the inside of each ear
make two tufts. For the eyes, use ki yarn to
make elongated French knots. Work each
knot over 2 sts at a slight angle and wrap
the yarn around the needle five times. With
bl yarn, make a stitch over the center of the
French knot. For whiskers, cut 3in (8cm)
strands of sewing thread and thread
through cheeks, then trim.

Tail

You could use a pipecleaner to shape
the curved tail, but this is not vital.

Ear

(make 2 the same)
With US 2 (2¾mm) needles and cn, cast on
5 sts.
Beg with a k row, work 3 rows st st.
Row 4: P2tog, p1, p2tog. *(3 sts)*
Work 2 rows st st.
Row 7: K3tog and fasten off.

Abyssinian Cat Sitting

To give the impression of a ticked coat, our Abyssinian is knitted in flecked yarn.

Measurements

Length: 7in (18cm)
Height to top of head: 4¾in (12cm)

Materials

- Pair of US 2 (2¾mm) knitting needles
- 2 spare US 2 (2¾mm) knitting needles or small stitch holders or safety pins
- Pair of US 2 (2¾mm) double-pointed knitting needles
- ½oz (15g) of Rowan Felted Tweed in Cinnamon 175 (cn)
- ⅛oz (5g) of Rowan Pure Wool 4ply in Porcelaine 451 (pr)
- Tiny amount of Rowan Cashsoft 4ply in Bark 432 (bk)
- Tiny amount of Rowan Cashsoft 4ply in Kiwi 443 (ki) for eyes
- Tiny amount of Rowan Pure Wool 4ply in Black 404 (bl) for pupils
- 2 pipecleaners
- Crochet hook
- Cream sewing thread for whiskers

Abbreviations

See page 141.
See page 141 for Wrap Method.
See page 141 for Stranding or Fair Isle Technique.

Back Leg

(make 2 the same)
With US 2 (2¾mm) needles and cn, cast on 7 sts.
Work 6 rows st st.
Row 7: K1, inc into next 2 sts, k1, inc into next 2 sts, k1. *(11 sts)*
Row 8: Purl.
Row 9: K1, inc into next 4 sts, k1, inc into next 4 sts, k1. *(19 sts)*
Row 10: Purl.
Row 11: K7, inc into next 2 sts, k1, inc into next 2 sts, k7. *(23 sts)*
Row 12: Purl.
Row 13: K9, inc into next 2 sts, k1, inc into next 2 sts, k9. *(27 sts)*
Work 5 rows st st.
Row 19: [K2tog] twice, k19, [k2tog] twice. *(23 sts)*
Row 20: [P2tog] twice, p15, [p2tog] twice. *(19 sts)*

Legs

Lightly stuff the legs to keep them looking slim and elegant.

Row 21: [K2tog] twice, k11, [k2tog] twice. *(15 sts)*
Row 22: Purl.
Row 23: [K2tog] twice, k7, [k2tog] twice. *(11 sts)*
Row 24: Purl.
Row 25: [K2tog] twice, k3, [k2tog] twice. *(7 sts)* Bind off.

Right Front Leg

With US 2 (2¾mm) needles and cn, cast on 7 sts.
Work 2 rows st st.
Row 3: Inc, k2tog, k1, k2tog, inc. *(7 sts)*
Row 4: Purl. Rep last 2 rows once more.
Work 8 rows st st.
Row 15: Inc, k5, inc. *(9 sts)*
Row 16: Purl.
Row 17: K2tog, k1, inc, k1, inc, k1, k2tog. *(9 sts)*
Row 18: Purl.*
Row 19: Bind off 4 sts, k to end (hold 5 sts on spare needle for Right Side of Body).

Left Front Leg

Work as for Right Front Leg to *.
Row 19: K5, bind off 4 sts (hold 5 sts on spare needle of Left Side of Body).

Right Side of Body

With US 2 (2¾mm) needles and cn, cast on 5 sts.
Beg with a k row, work 2 rows st st.
Row 3: Inc, k4. *(6 sts)*
Row 4: Purl.
Row 5: Inc, k5. *(7 sts)*
Row 6: Purl.
Row 7: K6, inc. *(8 sts)*
Row 8: Purl.
Row 9: Inc, k7. *(9 sts)*
Row 10: Purl.
Row 11: Knit.
Row 12: Purl.
Row 13: Inc, k6, k2tog. *(9 sts)*

Row 14: P9, cast on 2 sts, p5 from spare needle of Right Front Leg, cast on 2 sts. *(18 sts)*
Row 15: Knit.
Row 16: Purl.
Row 17: K16, k2tog. *(17 sts)*
Row 18: Purl.
Row 19: Inc, k16. *(18 sts)*
Row 20: Purl.
Row 21: K16, k2tog. *(17 sts)*
Row 22: Purl.
Row 23: Inc, k14, k2tog. *(17 sts)*
Row 24: Purl.
Row 25: Inc, k14, k2tog. *(17 sts)*
Row 26: P15, p2tog. *(16 sts)*
Row 27: K14, k2tog. *(15 sts)*
Row 28: Bind off 4 sts, p to end (hold 11 sts on spare needle for Neck).

Left Side of Body

With US 2 (2¾mm) needles and cn, cast on 5 sts.
Beg with a p row, work 2 rows st st.
Row 3: Inc, p4. *(6 sts)*
Row 4: Knit.
Row 5: Inc, p5. *(7 sts)*
Row 6: Knit.
Row 7: P6, inc. *(8 sts)*
Row 8: Knit.
Row 9: Inc, p7. *(9 sts)*
Row 10: Knit.
Row 11: Purl.
Row 12: Knit.
Row 13: Inc, p6, p2tog. *(9 sts)*
Row 14: K9, cast on 2 sts, k5 from spare needle of Left Front Leg, cast on 2 sts. *(18 sts)*
Row 15: Purl.
Row 16: Knit.
Row 17: P16, p2tog. *(17 sts)*
Row 18: Knit.
Row 19: Inc, p16. *(18 sts)*
Row 20: Knit.
Row 21: P16, p2tog. *(17 sts)*
Row 22: Knit.

Row 23: Inc, p14, p2tog. *(17 sts)*
Row 24: Knit.
Row 25: Inc, p14, p2tog. *(17 sts)*
Row 26: K15, k2tog. *(16 sts)*
Row 27: P14, p2tog. *(15 sts)*
Row 28: Bind off 4 sts, k to end (hold 11 sts on spare needle for Neck).

Neck and Head

Row 1: With US 2 (2¾mm) needles and RS facing, k8 sts, k2tog, k1 from spare needle of Right Side of Body, then k1, k2tog, k8 from spare needle of Left Side of Body. *(20 sts)*
Row 2: P2tog, p5, p2tog, p2, p2tog, p5, p2tog. *(16 sts)*
Row 3: K5, k2tog, k2, k2tog, k5. *(14 sts)*
Row 4: Purl.
Row 5: K4, k2tog, k2, k2tog, k4. *(12 sts)*
Row 6: P2tog, p8, p2tog. *(10 sts)*
Row 7: Inc, k8, inc. *(12 sts)*
Row 8: Inc, p10, inc. *(14 sts)*
Row 9: K12, wrap and turn.
Row 10: P10, w&t.
Row 11: K10, w&t.
Rep last 2 rows once more.
Row 14: P10, w&t.
Row 15: K12.
Row 16: P14.
Row 17: K12, wrap and turn.
Join in bk.
Row 18: P3cn, k4bk, p3cn, w&t.
Row 19: K3cn, k4bk, k3cn, w&t.
Row 20: P2cn, p1bk, p4cn, p1bk, p2cn, w&t.
Row 21: K2cn, k1bk, k1cn, k2bk, k1cn, k1bk, k2cn, w&t.
Row 22: P2bk, p2cn, p2bk, p2cn, p2bk, w&t.
Cont in cn.
Row 23: K12.
Row 24: P2tog, p1, [p2tog] 4 times, p1, p2tog. *(8 sts)*
Row 25: K1, k2tog, k2, k2tog, k1. *(6 sts)*
Row 26: Purl.
Row 27: K2tog, k2, k2tog. *(4 sts)*
Bind off.

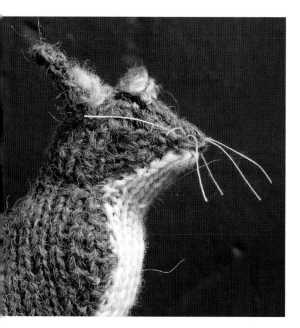

Head

The ears have characteristic tufts that are made from strands of yarn hooked through the knitting.

Tummy

With US 2 (2¾mm) needles and pr, cast on 3 sts.
Beg with a k row, work 8 rows st st.
Row 9: Inc, k1, inc. *(5 sts)*
Work 7 rows st st.
Row 17: Inc, k3, inc. *(7 sts)*
Work 7 rows st st.
Row 25: K2tog, k3, k2tog. *(5 sts)*
Row 26: P2tog, p1, p2tog. *(3 sts)*
Work 4 rows st st.
Row 31: Inc, k1, inc. *(5 sts)*
Work 23 rows st st.
Row 55: K2tog, k1, k2tog. *(3 sts)*
Work 4 rows st st.
Row 60: P3tog and fasten off.

Ear

(make 2 the same)
With US 2 (2¾mm) needles and cn, cast on 5 sts.
Work 3 rows st st.
Row 4: P2tog, p1, p2tog. *(3 sts)*
Work 2 rows st st.
Row 7: K3tog and fasten off.

Tail

With US 2 (2¾mm) double-pointed needles and cn, cast on 7 sts.
Work in i-cord as follows:
Knit 10 rows.
Row 11: K2tog, k3, k2tog. *(5 sts)*
Knit 16 rows.
Row 28: K2tog, k1, k2tog. *(3 sts)*
Row 29: K3tog and fasten off.

To Finish

Sew in ends, leaving ends from bound off rows for sewing up. Using mattress or whip stitch, sew up legs starting at paw. Cut a pipecleaner to fit length of back leg, fold over the ends (so they don't poke out of the paws), and slip into leg. Lightly stuff and sew along top of back legs, then bend into shape as shown in photograph. Using mattress or whip stitch, sew along back of cat. At head, fold in half and sew bound off edges of nose together. Using mattress or whip stitch, sew cast on row of tummy to bottom end of cat and sew final row to nose. Ease and sew tummy to fit body, matching curves to front legs. Leave a 1in (2.5cm) gap on one side. Roll a pipecleaner in a small amount of stuffing and bend into a U shape. Fold over the ends (so they don't poke out of the paws) and slip into body down front legs. Stuff, and sew up gap with mattress stitch. Using whip stitch, attach back legs to body, sewing along top of leg and down back edge as shown in photograph. To hold the legs in place, at about ½in (1cm) down from top of leg, sew the inside of the leg to the body. Mold into shape. Attach the tail as in photograph. Sew ears to head, leaving about 3 sts between the two ears. Using a crochet hook and 2 strands of unplied pr yarn, on the inside of each ear make two tufts. For the eyes, use ki yarn to make elongated French knots. Work each knot over 2 sts at a slight angle and wrap the yarn around the needle five times. With bl yarn, make a stitch over the center of the French knot. For whiskers, cut 3in (8cm) strands of sewing thread and thread through cheeks, then trim.

Burmese

A dog in cat's clothing, the Burmese is doglike in its love of fetching and game-playing. Very affectionate and friendly, Burmese are also one of the more vocal cats. All Burmese are allegedly descended from a single cat, Wong Mau; found in Burma in 1930, she was brought back to San Francisco and bred with a Siamese. We grew up with a series of Burmese cats—Kettering (brown), Monty (blue), Lumio (red), and Nestles (brown).

Burmese Cat Sitting

The Burmese is one of the simpler cats to knit, being just one color with no loops.

Measurements

Length: 5½in (14cm)
Height to top of head: 5¼in (13cm)

Materials

- Pair of US 2 (2¾mm) knitting needles
- 2 spare US 2 (2¾mm) knitting needles or small stitch holders or safety pins
- Pair of US 2 (2¾mm) double-pointed knitting needles
- 1oz (20g) of Rowan Pure Wool 4ply in Mocha 417 (mo)
- Tiny amount of Rowan Pure Wool 4ply in Black 404 (bl) for nose
- Tiny amount of Rowan Cashsoft 4ply in Almond 458 (al) for eyes
- 2 pipecleaners
- Transparent nylon thread for whiskers

Abbreviations

See page 141.
See page 141 for Wrap Method.

Back Leg

(make 2 the same)
With US 2 (2¾mm) needles and mo, cast on 9 sts.
Beg with a k row, work 10 rows st st.
Row 11: K1, inc into next 2 sts, k3, inc into next 2 sts, k1. *(13 sts)*
Row 12: Purl.

Row 13: K1, inc into next 4 sts, k3, inc into next 4 sts, k1. *(21 sts)*
Row 14: Purl.
Row 15: K7, inc into next 2 sts, k3, inc into next 2 sts, k7. *(25 sts)*
Row 16: Purl.
Row 17: K9, inc into next 2 sts, k3, inc into next 2 sts, k9. *(29 sts)*
Work 5 rows st st.
Row 23: [K2tog] 3 times, k17, [k2tog] 3 times. *(23 sts)*
Row 24: [P2tog] twice, p15, [p2tog] twice. *(19 sts)*
Row 25: [K2tog] twice, k11, [k2tog] twice. *(15 sts)*
Row 26: Purl.
Row 27: [K2tog] twice, k7, [k2tog] twice. *(11 sts)*
Row 28: Purl.
Row 29: [K2tog] twice, k3, [k2tog] twice. *(7 sts)*
Row 30: Purl.
Bind off.

Right Front Leg

With US 2 (2¾mm) needles and mo, cast on 9 sts.
Beg with a k row, work 2 rows st st.
Row 3: Inc, k1, k2tog, k1, k2tog, k1, inc. *(9 sts)*
Row 4: Purl.
Rep last 2 rows once more.
Work 6 rows st st.
Row 13: Inc, k7, inc. *(11 sts)*
Row 14: Purl.
Row 15: Inc, k9, inc. *(13 sts)*
Row 16: Purl.
Row 17: Inc, k11, inc. *(15 sts)*
Work 5 rows st st.*
Row 23: Bind off 7 sts, k to end (hold 8 sts on spare needle for Right Front Leg).

Left Front Leg

Work as for Right Front Leg to *.
Row 23: K8, bind off 7 sts (hold 8 sts on spare needle for Left Front Leg).

Right Side of Body

With US 2 (2¾mm) needles and mo, cast on 5 sts.
Beg with a k row, work 4 rows st st.
Row 5: Inc, k4. *(6 sts)*
Row 6: Purl.
Row 7: Inc, k5. *(7 sts)*
Row 8: Purl.
Row 9: Inc, k6. *(8 sts)*
Row 10: Purl.
Row 11: Inc, k7. *(9 sts)*
Row 12: Purl.
Row 13: Inc, k8. *(10 sts)*
Row 14: Purl.
Row 15: Inc, k9. *(11 sts)*
Row 16: Purl.
Row 17: Inc, k10. *(12 sts)*
Row 18: Purl.
Row 19: Inc, k11. *(13 sts)*
Row 20: Purl.
Row 21: Inc, k12. *(14 sts)*
Row 22: P14, with WS facing p8 from spare needle of Right Front Leg, cast on 1 st. *(23 sts)*
Work 3 rows st st.
Row 26: P2tog, p21. *(22 sts)*
Row 27: Knit.
Row 28: P2tog, p20. *(21 sts)*
Row 29: Inc, k20. *(22 sts)*
Row 30: P2tog, p20. *(21 sts)*
Row 31: K19, k2tog. *(20 sts)*
Row 32: P2tog, p18. *(19 sts)*
Row 33: K17, k2tog. *(18 sts)*
Row 34: P2tog, p16. *(17 sts)*
Row 35: K15, k2tog. *(16 sts)*
Row 36: Bind off 4 sts, p to end. *(12 sts)*
Row 37: K2tog, k8, k2tog. *(10 sts)*
Row 38: P2tog, p8. *(9 sts)*
Row 39: K7, k2tog. *(8 sts)*

Row 17: Inc, p10. *(12 sts)*
Row 18: Knit.
Row 19: Inc, p11. *(13 sts)*
Row 20: Knit.
Row 21: Inc, p12. *(14 sts)*
Row 22: K14, with RS facing k8 from spare needle of Left Front Leg, cast on 1 st. *(23 sts)* Work 3 rows st st.
Row 26: K2tog, k21. *(22 sts)*
Row 27: Purl.
Row 28: K2tog, k20. *(21 sts)*
Row 29: Inc, p20. *(22 sts)*
Row 30: K2tog, k20. *(21 sts)*
Row 31: P19, p2tog. *(20 sts)*
Row 32: K2tog, k18. *(19 sts)*
Row 33: P17, p2tog. *(18 sts)*
Row 34: K2tog, k16. *(17 sts)*
Row 35: P15, p2tog. *(16 sts)*
Row 36: Bind off 4 sts, k to end. *(12 sts)*
Row 37: P2tog, p8, p2tog. *(10 sts)*
Row 38: K2tog, k8. *(9 sts)*
Row 39: P7, p2tog. *(8 sts)*
Row 40: K8 (hold 8 sts on spare needle for Neck).

Neck and Head

Row 1: With US 2 (2¾mm) needles and mo and RS facing, k8 from spare needle of Right Side of Body, then k8 from spare needle of Left Side of Body. *(16 sts)*
Row 2: Inc, p14, inc. *(18 sts)*
Row 3: [Inc] twice, k14, [inc] twice. *(22 sts)*
Row 4: Inc, p20, inc. *(24 sts)*
Row 5: Inc, k16, wrap and turn.
Row 6: P10, w&t.
Row 7: K10, w&t.
Row 8: P10, w&t.
Row 9: K16, inc. *(26 sts)*
Row 10: Purl.
Row 11: K17, wrap and turn.
Row 12: P8, w&t.
Row 13: K8, w&t.
Row 14: P8, w&t.
Row 15: K across all sts. *(26 sts)*

Body

The Burmese has a slight, delicate body that doesn't take long to knit. All the sitting cats have back legs knitted separately and sewn on.

Row 40: P8 (hold 8 sts on spare needle for Neck).

Left Side of Body

With US 2 (2¾mm) needles and mo, cast on 5 sts.
Beg with a p row, work 4 rows st st.
Row 5: Inc, p4. *(6 sts)*
Row 6: Knit.
Row 7: Inc, p5. *(7 sts)*
Row 8: Knit.
Row 9: Inc, p6. *(8 sts)*
Row 10: Knit.
Row 11: Inc, p7. *(9 sts)*
Row 12: Knit.
Row 13: Inc, p8. *(10 sts)*
Row 14: Knit.
Row 15: Inc, p9. *(11 sts)*
Row 16: Knit.

Head

This Burmese has round French knots for eyes. You can give your cat elongated, slanting eyes if you prefer.

Row 16: [P2tog, p2] 6 times, p2tog. *(19 sts)*
Row 17: [K2tog] 4 times, k3, [k2tog] 4 times. *(11 sts)*
Row 18: [P2tog] twice, p3, [p2tog] twice. *(7 sts)*
Row 19: K2tog, k3, k2tog. *(5 sts)*
Row 20: P2tog, p1, p2tog. *(3 sts)*
Bind off.

Tummy

With US 2 (2¾mm) needles and mo, cast on 3 sts.
Beg with a k row, work 8 rows st st.
Row 9: Inc, k1, inc. *(5 sts)*
Work 37 rows st st.
Row 47: K2tog, k1, k2tog. *(3 sts)*
Work 15 rows st st.
Row 63: Inc, k1, inc. *(5 sts)*
Row 64: Purl.
Row 65: K2tog, k1, k2tog. *(3 sts)*
Bind off.

Ear

(make 2 the same)
With US 2 (2¾mm) needles and mo, cast on 6 sts.
Beg with a k row, work 4 rows st st.
Row 5: K2tog, k2, k2tog. *(4 sts)*
Row 6: Purl.
Row 7: [K2tog] twice. *(2 sts)*
Row 8: P2tog and fasten off.

Tail

With US 2 (2¾mm) double-pointed needles and mo, cast on 5 sts.
Work in i-cord as follows:
Knit 28 rows.
Row 29: K2tog, k1, k2tog. *(3 sts)*
Row 30: K2tog, k1. *(2 sts)*
Row 31: K2tog and fasten off.

To Finish

Sew in ends, leaving ends from bound off rows for sewing up. Using mattress or whip stitch, sew up legs starting at paw. Using mattress or whip stitch, sew along back of cat. Using mattress or whip stitch, sew cast on row of tummy to bottom end of cat and sew bound off row to nose. Ease and sew tummy to fit body. Leave a 1in (2.5cm) gap on one side. Turn right side out. Roll a pipecleaner in a small amount of stuffing and bend into a U shape. Fold over the ends (so they don't poke out of the paws) and slip into body down front legs. Stuff, and sew up gap with mattress stitch. Cut a pipecleaner to fit length of back leg, fold over the ends, and slip into leg. Lightly stuff and sew along top of back legs, then bend into shape as shown in photograph. Using whip stitch and with seams at back, attach back legs to body, sewing along top of leg and down back edge as shown in photograph. To hold the legs in place, at about ½in (1cm) down from top of leg, sew through the leg, body, and opposite leg on inside. Mold into shape. Attach the tail, which can be positioned curled up or to the side. Sew ears to head, leaving about 3 sts between the two ears. For the eyes, use al yarn to make round French knots. Work each knot over 2 sts and wrap the yarn around the needle four times, push needle back through same hole, and sew down with a small stitch at bottom of knot to form a circle. With bl yarn, make a stitch over the center of the French knot. For nose, use bl yarn to embroider three parallel lines at point of nose, two long and one short. For whiskers, cut three 3in (8cm) strands of transparent nylon and thread through cheeks, then trim.

Blue Burmese

We have made the Blue Burmese in silk yarn to give him a characteristic extra-silky look.

Measurements
Length: 6in (15cm)
Height to top of head: 5½in (14cm)

Materials
- Pair of US 2 (2¾mm) knitting needles
- 4 spare US 2 (2¾mm) knitting needles or small stitch holders or safety pins
- Pair of US 2 (2¾mm) double-pointed knitting needles
- 1oz (20g) of Rowan Classic Pure Silk DK in Tranquil 156 (tr)
- Tiny amount of Rowan Pure Wool 4ply in Black 404 (bl) for nose
- Tiny amount of Rowan Cashsoft 4ply in Almond 458 (al) for eyes
- 2 pipecleaners
- White sewing thread for whiskers

Abbreviations
See page 141.
See page 141 for Wrap Method.

Right Back Leg
With US 2 (2¾mm) needles and tr, cast on 9 sts.
Beg with a k row, work 2 rows st st.
Row 3: Inc, k2tog, k3, k2tog, inc. *(9 sts)*
Row 4: Purl.
Rep last 2 rows once more,
Work 4 rows st st.

Row 11: K2, inc, k3, inc, k2. *(11 sts)*
Row 12 and every alt row: Purl.
Row 13: K2, inc, k5, inc, k2. *(13 sts)*
Row 15: K2tog, inc, k7, inc, k2tog. *(13 sts)*
Row 17: K2tog, inc, k1, inc, k3, inc, k1, inc, k2tog. *(15 sts)*
Row 19: K3, inc, k7, inc, k3. *(17 sts)*
Row 21: K3, inc, k9, inc, k3. *(19 sts)*
Row 23: K3, inc, k11, inc, k3. *(21 sts)*
Row 25: K3, inc, k13, inc, k3. *(23 sts)*
Row 26: Purl.*
Row 27: Bind off 11 sts, k to end (hold 12 sts on spare needle for Right Side of Body).

Left Back Leg
Work as for Right Back Leg to *.
Row 27: K12, bind off 11 sts (hold 12 sts on spare needle for Left Side of Body).

Right Front Leg
With US 2 (2¾mm) needles and tr, cast on 9 sts.
Beg with a k row, work 2 rows st st.
Row 3: Inc, k2tog, k3, k2tog, inc. *(9 sts)*
Row 4: Purl.
Rep last 2 rows once more.
Work 6 rows st st.
Row 13: Inc, k7, inc. *(11 sts)*
Work 3 rows st st.
Row 17: K3, inc, k3, inc, k3. *(13 sts)*
Row 18 and every alt row: Purl.
Row 19: K4, inc, k3, inc, k4. *(15 sts)*
Row 21: K5, inc, k3, inc, k5.** *(17 sts)*
Row 23: Bind off 8 sts, k to end (hold 9 sts on spare needle for Right Side of Body).

Left Front Leg
Work as for Right Front Leg to **.
Row 23: K9, bind off 8 sts (hold 9 sts on spare needle for Left Side of Body).

Right Side of Body
Row 1: With US 2 (2¾mm) needles and tr, cast on 1 st, with RS facing k9 from spare needle of Right Front Leg. *(10 sts)*
Row 2: Purl.
Row 3: Inc, k9, cast on 7 sts. *(18 sts)*
Row 4: Purl.
Row 5: Inc, k17, cast on 6 sts, with RS facing k12 from spare needle of Right Back Leg. *(37 sts)*
Work 5 rows st st.
Row 11: K35, k2tog. *(36 sts)*
Work 3 rows st st.
Row 15: K2tog, k34. *(35 sts)*
Row 16: P2tog, p33. *(34 sts)*
Work 3 rows st st.
Row 20: P3 (hold these 3 sts on spare needle for Tail), bind off 23 sts, p to end (hold rem 8 sts on spare needle for Neck).

Left Side of Body
Row 1: With US 2 (2¾mm) needles and tr, cast on 1 st, with WS facing p9 from spare needle of Left Front Leg. *(10 sts)*
Row 2: Knit.
Row 3: Inc, p9, cast on 7 sts. *(18 sts)*
Row 4: Knit.
Row 5: Inc, p17, cast on 6 sts, with WS facing p12 from spare needle of Left Back Leg. *(37 sts)*
Work 5 rows st st.
Row 11: P35, p2tog. *(36 sts)*
Work 3 rows st st.
Row 15: P2tog, p34. *(35 sts)*
Row 16: K2tog, k33. *(34 sts)*
Work 3 rows st st.
Row 20: K3 (hold these 3 sts on spare needle for Tail), bind off 23 sts, k to end (hold rem 8 sts on spare needle for Neck).

Neck and Head
Row 1: With US 2 (2¾mm) needles and tr and RS facing, k8 from spare needle of Right Side of Body, then k8 from spare needle of Left Side of Body. *(16 sts)*

Head

The gleaming green eyes don't have pupils, but you can add a black stitch across the French knots if you want.

Row 2: Inc, p14, inc. *(18 sts)*
Row 3: [Inc] twice, k14, [inc] twice. *(22 sts)*
Row 4: Inc, p20, inc. *(24 sts)*
Row 5: Inc, k16, wrap and turn.
Row 6: P10, w&t.
Row 7: K10, w&t.
Row 8: P10, w&t.
Row 9: K16, inc. *(26 sts)*
Row 10: Purl.
Row 11: K17, wrap and turn.
Row 12: P8, w&t.
Row 13: K8, w&t.
Row 14: P8, w&t.
Row 15: K across all sts. *(26 sts)*
Row 16: [P2tog, p2] 6 times, p2tog. *(19 sts)*
Row 17: [K2tog] 4 times, k3, [k2tog] 4 times. *(11 sts)*
Row 18: [P2tog] twice, p3, [p2tog] twice. *(7 sts)*
Row 19: K2tog, k3, k2tog. *(5 sts)*
Row 20: P2tog, p1, p2tog. *(3 sts)*
Row 21: K3tog and fasten off.

Tummy

With US 2 (2¾mm) needles and tr, cast on 6 sts.
Beg with a k row, work 14 rows st st.
Row 15: Inc, k4, inc. *(8 sts)*
Work 19 rows st st.
Row 35: K2tog, k4, k2tog. *(6 sts)*
Work 35 rows st st.
Row 71: K2tog, k2, k2tog. *(4 sts)*
Row 72: [P2tog] twice. *(2 sts)*
Row 73: K2tog and fasten off.

Ear

(make 2 the same)
With US 2 (2¾mm) needles and tr, cast on 6 sts.
Beg with a k row, work 4 rows st st.
Row 5: K2tog, k2, k2tog. *(4 sts)*
Row 6: Purl.
Row 7: [K2tog] twice. *(2 sts)*
Row 8: P2tog and fasten off.

Tail

With US 2 (2¾mm) double-pointed needles and tr and RS facing, k3 from spare needle for Left Side of Body for Tail, then k3 from spare needle for Right Side of Body for Tail. *(6 sts)*
Work in i-cord as follows:
Knit 10 rows.
Row 11: K2, k2tog, k2. *(4 sts)*
Knit 12 rows.
Row 24: [K2tog] twice. *(2 sts)*
Row 25: K2tog and fasten off.

To Finish

Sew in ends, leaving ends from bound off rows for sewing up. Using mattress or whip stitch, sew up legs starting at paw. Using mattress or whip stitch, sew along back of cat and down bottom. Using mattress or whip stitch, sew cast on row of tummy to bottom end of cat and sew final row to nose. Ease and sew tummy to fit body. Leave a 1in (2.5cm) gap between front and back legs on one side. Roll the pipecleaners in a small amount of stuffing and bend each one into a U shape. Fold over the ends (so they don't poke out of the paws) and slip into body, one pipecleaner down front legs and one down back legs. Stuff, and sew up gap with mattress stitch. Mold into shape. Sew ears to head, leaving about 3 sts between the two ears. For the eyes, use al yarn to make round French knots. Work each knot over 2 sts and wrap the yarn around the needle four times, push needle back through same hole, and sew down with a small stitch at bottom of knot to form a circle. For nose, use bl yarn to embroider three parallel lines at point of nose, two long and one short. For whiskers, cut 3in (8cm) strands of sewing thread and thread through cheeks, then trim.

H.A.Jones&C.º

Bengal

The living room leopard, the Bengal is the result of a 'Mowgli complex'—the desire to have a small-scale version of a wild cat in your own home—but you have to pay for it. One of the most expensive cats in the world, a Bengal was bought for £25,320 (around $41,000) in 1998. Reportedly, these showstopping cats are sometimes seen out and about on leashes or on the shoulders of their famous owners, who include Kevin Bacon, Jeffrey Archer, and Paris Hilton.

Bengal

The Bengal is a complex but rewarding cat to knit.

Measurements

Length: 10in (25cm)
Height to top of head: 4½in (11cm)

Materials

- Pair of US 2 (2¾mm) knitting needles
- 4 spare US 2 (2¾mm) knitting needles or small stitch holders or safety pins
- Pair of US 2 (2¾mm) double-pointed knitting needles
- ⅛oz (5g) of Rowan Cashsoft 4ply in Black 422 (bl)
- 1oz (20g) of Rowan Cashsoft 4ply in Savannah 439 (sa)
- ⅛oz (5g) of Rowan Pure Wool 4ply in Toffee 453 (tf)
- ⅛oz (5g) of Rowan Kidsilk Haze in Cream 634 (cr) used DOUBLE throughout
- Small amount of Rowan Cashsoft 4ply in Amethyst 444 (am)
- Tiny amount of Rowan Cashsoft 4ply in Fennel 436 (fn) for eyes
- Tiny amount of Rowan Pure Wool 4ply in Powder 443 (po) for nose
- 2 pipecleaners
- Crochet hook
- Cream sewing thread for whiskers

Abbreviations

See page 141.
See page 141 for Wrap Method.
See page 141 for Stranding or Fair Isle Technique.

Left Back Leg

With US 2 (2¾mm) needles and sa, cast on 7 sts.
Row 1: Knit.
Join in bl.
Row 2: P2sa, p3bl, p2sa.
Row 3: Incsa, k2togbl, k1bl, k2togbl, incsa. *(7 sts)*
Row 4: P3sa, p1bl, p3sa.
Row 5: Incsa, k2togsa, k1sa, k2togsa, incsa. *(7 sts)*
Row 6: Purl in sa.*
Work 2 rows st st in sa.
Row 9: K2sa, incsa, k1sa, incbl, k2bl. *(9 sts)*
Row 10: P4sa, p3bl, p2sa.
Row 11: K2togbl, inc into next 2 sts bl, k1sa, inc into next 2 sts sa, k2togsa. *(11 sts)*
Cont in sa.
Row 12: P2tog, p2, inc, p1, inc, p2, p2tog. *(11 sts)*
Row 13: K2tog, inc, k1, inc, k1, inc, k1, inc, k2tog. *(13 sts)***
Join in bl.
Row 14: P2sa, p4bl, p7sa.
Row 15: K3sa, incbl, k1bl, incbl, k1bl, incsa, k1sa, incsa, k3sa. *(17 sts)*
Row 16: P14sa, p3bl.
Row 17: K7sa, incsa, k1sa, incsa, k7sa. *(19 sts)*
Row 18: P5bl, p14sa.
Row 19: K8sa, incbl, k1bl, incbl, k3bl, k5sa. *(21 sts)*
Row 20: P13sa, p4bl, p4sa.
Row 21: K2sa, k2bl, k5sa, incsa, k1sa, incsa, k9sa. *(23 sts)*
Row 22: P7sa, p5bl, p9sa, p2bl.
Row 23: K6sa, k5bl, k12sa.
Row 24: P17sa, p3bl, p3sa.
Row 25: K3bl, k9sa, bind off 11 sts sa (hold 12 sts on spare needle for Left Side of Body).

Right Back Leg

Work as for Left Back Leg to **.
Join in bl.

Row 14: P9sa, p4bl.
Row 15: K4sa, k1bl, incbl, k1bl, incbl, k4bl, wrap and turn.
Row 16: P4bl, p9sa, w&t.
Row 17: K5sa, incsa, k1sa, incsa, k4sa, w&t. *(14 sts)*
Row 18: P10sa, p3bl, w&t.
Row 19: K3sa, k2bl, incbl, k1bl, incsa, k7sa. *(19 sts in total)*
Row 20: P5sa, p4bl, p10sa.
Row 21: K8sa, incsa, k1sa, incsa, k3sa, k3bl, k2sa. *(21 sts)*
Row 22: P2bl, p19sa.
Row 23: K9sa, incsa, k1sa, incsa, k9sa. *(23 sts)*
Row 24: P9sa, p5bl, p9sa.
Row 25: K14sa, k4bl, k5sa.
Row 26: P2sa, p3bl, p18sa.
Row 27: Bind off 11 sts sa, k10sa ibos, k2bl (hold 12 sts on spare needle for Right Side of Body).

Right Front Leg

With US 2 (2¾mm) needles and sa, cast on 7 sts. Work as for Left Back Leg to *.
Row 7: Knit in sa.
Row 8: P4sa, p3bl.
Row 9: K3sa, k2bl, k2sa.
Row 10: P2bl, p5sa.
Work 2 rows st st in sa.
Row 13: Incbl, k1bl, k4sa, incsa. *(9 sts)*
Row 14: P7bl, p2sa.
Row 15: K3sa, incsa, k1sa, incsa, k3bl. *(11 sts)*
Row 16: P8sa, p3bl.
Row 17: K3sa, k1bl, incbl, k1sa, incsa, k4sa. *(13 sts)*
Row 18: P4sa, p3bl, p6sa.
Row 19: K5sa, incsa, k1sa, incsa, k3bl, k2sa. *(15 sts)*
Row 20: P3bl, p12sa.
Row 21: K6sa, incsa, k1bl, incbl, k1bl, k5sa. *(17 sts)*
Row 22: P4sa, p3bl, p10sa.

Legs

Bend the legs to exaggerate the prowling pose—the slinkier, the better.

Row 23: Bind off 8 sts, k4sa ibos, k2bl, k3sa (hold 9 sts on spare needle for Right Side of Body).

Left Front Leg

Work as for Left Back Leg to *.
Row 7: Knit in sa.
Row 8: P3bl, p4sa.
Row 9: K2sa, k2bl, k3sa.
Row 10: P5sa, p2bl.
Work 2 rows st st in sa.
Row 13: Incsa, k4sa, k1bl, incbl. (9 sts)
Row 14: P2sa, p7bl.
Row 15: K3bl, incsa, k1sa, incsa, k3sa. (11 sts)
Row 16: P3bl, p8sa.
Row 17: K4sa, incsa, k1sa, incbl, k1bl, k3sa. (13 sts)
Row 18: P6sa, p3bl, p4sa.
Row 19: K2sa, k3bl, incsa, k1sa, incsa, k5sa. (15 sts)
Row 20: P12sa, p3bl.
Row 21: K5sa, k1bl, incbl, k1bl, incsa, k6sa. (17 sts)
Row 22: P10sa, p3bl, p4sa.
Row 23: K3sa, k2bl, k4sa, bind off 8 sts sa (hold 9 sts on spare needle for Left Side of Body).

Right Side of Body

Row 1: With US 2 (2¾mm) needles and sa, cast on 1 st, with RS facing k9 from spare needle of Right Front Leg, cast on 7 sts. (17 sts)
Join in bl.
Row 2: P5sa, p1bl, p2sa, p2bl, p2sa, p2bl, p2sa, incsa. (18 sts)
Row 3: Incsa, k10sa, k1bl, k6sa, cast on 8 sts sa. (27 sts)
Row 4: P7sa, p2bl, p2sa, p1bl, p3sa, p1bl, p3sa, p2bl, p5sa, incsa. (28 sts)
Join in tf.
Row 5: Incsa, k1sa, k1bl, k8sa, k1bl, k3sa, k1bl, k2sa, k1bl, k1tf, k1bl, k2sa, k2bl, k3sa, k12sa from spare needle of Right Back Leg, cast on 1 st sa. (42 sts)
Row 6: P5sa, p1bl, p3sa, p1bl, p7sa, p2bl, p2sa, p2bl, p4sa, p1bl, p2sa, p1bl, p6sa, p1bl, p3sa, incsa. (43 sts)
Row 7: Incsa, k2sa, k1bl, k2sa, k1bl, k4sa, k1bl, k3sa, k1bl, k16sa, k2bl, k4sa, k1bl, k4sa. (44 sts)
Row 8: P3sa, p1bl, p2sa, p1bl, p8sa, p1bl, p4sa, p2bl, p3sa, p1bl, p2sa, p1bl, p2sa, p1bl, p1sa, p1bl, p1tf, p2sa, p1bl, p2sa, p1bl, p2sa, incsa. (45 sts)
Row 9: Incsa, k5sa, k1bl, k3sa, k1tf, k1bl, k6sa, k2bl, k2sa, k1bl, k2tf, k1bl, k3sa, k2bl, k7sa, k2bl, k2sa, k1bl, k2sa. (46 sts)
Row 10: P13sa, p1bl, p2tf, p1bl, p2sa, p1bl, p2tf, p1bl, p2sa, p2bl, p7sa, p1bl, p1tf, p3sa, p1bl, p5sa, incsa. (47 sts)
Row 11: Incsa, k1bl, k2sa, k1bl, k1tf, k5sa, k1tf, k1bl, k7sa, k1bl, k4sa, k2bl, k4sa, k2bl, k4sa, k1bl, k9sa. (48 sts)
Row 12: P7sa, p1bl, p1tf, p1bl, p21sa, p1bl, p3sa, p1bl, p1tf, p4sa, p1tf, p1bl, p3sa, p1bl, incsa. (49 sts)
Row 13: K1sa, k1bl, k2sa, k1bl, k2sa, k1bl, k1tf, k3sa, k1tf, k1bl, k2sa, k1bl, k1tf, k1bl, k3sa, k1bl, k16sa, k1tf, k1bl, k3sa, k1bl, k4sa. (49 sts)
Row 14: P3sa, p1bl, p1tf, p1bl, p3sa, p1bl, p3sa, p1bl, p1tf, p4sa, p2bl, p4sa, p1bl, p1tf, p1bl, p2sa, p1bl, p1tf, p1bl, p3sa, p1bl, p1tf, p2sa, p1tf, p1bl, p2sa, p1bl, p2sa, p1bl, p1sa. (49 sts)
Row 15: K1sa, k1bl, k2sa, k1bl, k3sa, k1bl, k1tf, k1sa, k1tf, k1bl, k4sa, k1bl, k3sa, k1bl, k1tf, k1bl, k3sa, k1bl, k2tf, k1bl, k3sa, k1bl, k1tf, k1bl, k6sa, k1bl, k1f, k1bl, k1sa, k2togsa. (48 sts)
Row 16: P2togsa, p1sa, p1bl, p8sa, p1bl, p4sa, p1bl, p2tf, p1bl, p3sa, p2bl, p6sa, p1bl, p4sa, p1tf, p1bl, p3sa, p1bl, p5sa. (47 sts)
Row 17: K3sa, k1bl, k1sa, k1bl, k9sa, k1tf, k1bl, k11sa, k2bl, k15sa, k2togsa. (46 sts)
Bind off 46 sts sa.

Left Side of Body

Row 1: With US 2 (2¾mm) needles and sa, cast on 1 st, with WS facing p9 from spare needle of Left Front Leg, cast on 7 sts. *(17 sts)*
Join in bl.

Row 2: K5sa, k1bl, k2sa, k2bl, k2sa, k2bl, k2sa, incsa. *(18 sts)*

Row 3: Incsa, p10sa, p1bl, p6sa, cast on 8 sts sa. *(27 sts)*

Row 4: K7sa, k2bl, k2sa, k1bl, k3sa, k1bl, k3sa, k2bl, k5sa, incsa. *(28 sts)*
Join in tf.

Row 5: Incsa, p1sa, p1bl, p8sa, p1bl, p3sa, p1bl, p2sa, p1bl, p1tf, p1bl, p2sa, p2bl, p3sa, p12sa from spare needle of Left Back Leg, cast on 1 st sa. *(42 sts)*

Row 6: K5sa, k1bl, k3sa, k1bl, k7sa, k2bl, k2sa, k2bl, k4sa, k1bl, k2sa, k1bl, k6sa, k1bl, k3sa, incsa. *(43 sts)*

Row 7: Incsa, p2sa, p1bl, p2sa, p1bl, p4sa, p1bl, p3sa, p1bl, p16sa, p2bl, p4sa, p1bl, p4sa. *(44 sts)*

Row 8: K3sa, k1bl, k2sa, k1bl, k8sa, k1bl, k4sa, k2bl, k3sa, k1bl, k2sa, k1bl, k2sa, k1bl, k1sa, k1bl, k1tf, k2sa, k1bl, k2sa, k1bl, k2sa, incsa. *(45 sts)*

Row 9: Incsa, p5sa, p1bl, p3sa, p1tf, p1bl, p6sa, p2bl, p2sa, p1bl, p2tf, p1bl, p3sa, p2bl, p7sa, p2bl, p2sa, p1bl, p2sa. *(46 sts)*

Row 10: K13sa, k1bl, k2tf, k1bl, k2sa, k1bl, k2tf, k1bl, k2sa, k2bl, k7sa, k1bl, k1tf, k3sa, k1bl, k5sa, incsa. *(47 sts)*

Row 11: Incsa, p1bl, p2sa, p1bl, p1tf, p5sa, p1tf, p1bl, p7sa, p1bl, p4sa, p2bl, p4sa, p2bl, p4sa, p1bl, p9sa. *(48 sts)*

Row 12: K7sa, k1bl, k1tf, k1bl, k21sa, k1bl, k3sa, k1bl, k1tf, k4sa, k1tf, k1bl, k3sa, k1bl, incsa. *(49 sts)*

Row 13: P1sa, p1bl, p2sa, p1bl, p2sa, p1bl, p1tf, p3sa, p1tf, p1bl, p2sa, p1bl, p1tf, p1bl, p3sa, p1bl, p16sa, p1tf, p1bl, p3sa, p1bl, p4sa. *(49 sts)*

Row 14: K3sa, k1bl, k1tf, k1bl, k3sa, k1bl, k3sa, k1bl, k1tf, k4sa, k2bl, k4sa, k1bl, k1tf, k1bl, k2sa, k1bl, k1tf, k1bl, k3sa, k1bl, k1tf, k2sa, k1tf, k1bl, k2sa, k1bl, k2sa, k1bl, k1sa. *(49 sts)*

Row 15: P1sa, p1bl, p2sa, p1bl, p3sa, p1bl, p1tf, p1sa, p1tf, p1bl, p4sa, p1bl, p3sa, p1bl, p1tf, p1bl, p3sa, p1bl, p2tf, p1bl, p3sa, p1bl, p1tf, p1bl, p6sa, p1bl, p1tf, p1bl, p1sa, p2togsa. *(48 sts)*

Row 16: K2togsa, k1sa, k1bl, k8sa, k1bl, k4sa, k1bl, k1tf, k1bl, k3sa, k2bl, k6sa, k1bl, k5sa, k1tf, k1bl, k3sa, k1bl, k4sa. *(47 sts)*

Row 17: P3sa, p1bl, p1sa, p1bl, p9sa, p1tf, p1bl, p11sa, p2bl, p15sa, p2togsa. *(46 sts)*
Bind off 46 sts sa.

Neck and Head

Row 1: With US 2 (2¾mm) needles and sa, cast on 1 st, with RS facing pick up 7 sts from row ends at neck of Right Side of Body, then 7 sts from row ends at neck of Left Side of Body, cast on 1 st. *(16 sts)*
Join in bl.

Row 2: P5sa, p1bl, p1sa, p2bl, p1sa, p1bl, p5sa.

Row 3: Incsa, k3sa, k1bl, k2sa, k2bl, k2sa, k1bl, k3sa, incsa. *(18 sts)*

Row 4: Incsa, p2sa, p2bl, p3sa, p2bl, p3sa, p2bl, p2sa, incsa. *(20 sts)*

Row 5: K2sa, k2bl, k5sa, k2bl, k4sa, wrap and turn.

Row 6: P3sa, p1bl, p2sa, p1bl, p3sa, w&t.

Row 7: K3sa, k1bl, k2sa, k1bl, k3sa, w&t.

Row 8: P2sa, p1bl, p4sa, p1bl, p2sa, w&t.

Row 9: K2sa, k1bl, k4sa, k1bl, k2sa, w&t.

Row 10: P2sa, p1bl, p4sa, p1bl, p2sa, w&t.
Join in tf.

Row 11: K1sa, k1bl, k2sa, k2tf, k2sa, k1bl, k2sa, k2bl, k2sa. *(20 sts on right-hand needle)*

Row 12: P2bl, p4sa, p1bl, p2sa, p2tf, p2sa, p1bl, p4sa, p2bl.

Row 13: K5sa, k1bl, k1sa, k1bl, k1sa, k2tf, k1sa, k1bl, k1sa, k1bl, wrap and turn.

Row 14: P1bl, p1sa, p1bl, p1sa, p2tf, p1sa, p1bl, p1sa, p1bl, w&t.

Row 15: K1bl, k2sa, k1bl, k2tf, k1bl, k2sa, k1bl, w&t.

Row 16: P1sa, p1bl, p1sa, p1bl, p2tf, p1bl, p1sa, p1bl, p1sa, w&t.

Row 17: K1sa, k1bl, k1sa, k4tf, k1sa, k1bl, k6sa. *(20 sts on right-hand needle)*

Row 18: P2togsa, p1bl, p1sa, p2togsa, p2togbl, p2togtf, p2togtf, p2togbl, p2togsa, p1sa, p1bl, p2togsa. *(12 sts)*

Row 19: K2togbl, k2togsa, k2togtf, k2togtf, k2togsa, k2togbl. *(6 sts)*

Row 20: P2sa, p2togtf, p2sa. *(5 sts)*
Bind off 5 sts sa.

Head

The head is picked up from the body and the join is covered with the collar.

Tummy

With US 2 (2¾mm) needles and sa, cast on
5 sts.
Work 2 rows st st.
Change to cr.
Row 3: K2tog, k1, k2tog. *(3 sts)*
Work 11 rows st st.
Row 15: Inc, k1, inc. *(5 sts)*
Work 25 rows st st.
Row 41: K2tog, k1, k2tog. *(3 sts)*
Work 7 rows st st.
Row 49: Inc, k1, inc. *(5 sts)*
Work 7 rows st st.
Join in bl.
Row 57: K1cr, k1bl, k3cr.
Row 58: P2cr, p1bl, p2cr.
Work 2 rows st st cr.
Row 61: Inccr, k3cr, inccr. *(7 sts)*
Row 62: P1cr, p3bl, p3cr.
Work 1 row st st cr.
Row 64: P1cr, p1bl, p5cr.
Row 65: K4cr, k1bl, k2cr.
Row 66: P3cr, p2bl, p2cr.
Work 3 rows st st cr.
Row 70: P5cr, p1bl, p1cr.
Row 71: K2togcr, k2bl, k1cr, k2togcr. *(5 sts)*
Cont in cr.
Work 3 rows st st.
Row 75: K2tog, k1, k2tog. *(3 sts)*
Work 2 rows st st.
Row 78: P3tog and fasten off.

Left Ear

With US 2 (2¾mm) needles, cast on 3 sts sa,
cast on 2 sts bl. *(5 sts)*
Row 1: K2bl, k3sa.
Row 2: P3sa, p2bl.
Row 3: K2bl, k3sa.
Row 4: P2togsa, p1sa, p2togbl. *(3 sts)*
Row 5: K1bl, k2sa.
Row 6: P2sa, p1bl.
Row 7: K3togsa and fasten off.

Right Ear

With US 2 (2¾mm) needles, cast on 2 sts bl,
cast on 3 sts sa. *(5 sts)*
Row 1: K3sa, k2bl.
Row 2: P2bl, p3sa.
Row 3: K3sa, k2bl.
Row 4: P2togbl, p1sa, p2togsa. *(3 sts)*
Row 5: K2sa, k1bl.
Row 6: P1bl, p2sa.
Row 7: K3togsa and fasten off.

Tail

With US 2 (2¾mm) double-pointed needles
and sa, cast on 8 sts.
Work in i-cord as follows:
Knit 4 rows sa.
Join in bl.
Knit 1 row bl.
Knit 4 rows sa.
Knit 1 row bl.
Knit 3 rows sa.
Row 14: K2togbl, k4bl, k2togbl. *(6 sts)*
Knit 3 rows sa.
Knit 1 row bl.
Knit 3 rows sa.
Knit 1 row bl.
Knit 2 rows sa.
Knit 1 row bl.
Knit 1 row sa.
Row 27: K2togsa, k2sa, k2togsa. *(4 sts)*
Knit 1 row bl.
Knit 2 rows sa.
Knit 1 row bl.
Knit 2 rows sa.
Knit 1 row bl.
Knit 1 row sa.
Row 36: [K2togsa] twice. *(2 sts)*
Row 37: K2togsa and fasten off.

Collar

With US 2 (2¾mm) needles and am, cast on
24 sts.
Knit 1 row.
Bind off.

To Finish

Sew in ends, leaving ends from bound off
rows for sewing up. Using mattress or whip
stitch, sew up legs starting at paw. Using
mattress or whip stitch, sew along back of
cat and down bottom. At head, fold in half
and sew bound off edges of nose together.
Using mattress or whip stitch, sew cast on
row of tummy to bottom end of cat and sew
final row to nose. Ease and sew tummy to
fit body, matching curves to legs. Leave a
1in (2.5cm) gap between front and back
legs on one side. Roll the pipecleaners in
a small amount of stuffing and bend each
one into a U shape. Fold over the ends
(so they don't poke out of the paws) and
slip into body, one pipecleaner down front
legs and one down back legs. Stuff, and
sew up gap with mattress stitch. Mold into
shape. Attach the tail as in photograph.
Sew ears to head, leaving about 3 sts
between the two ears. Using a crochet hook
and 2 strands of cr yarn, on the inside of
each ear make two tufts. For the eyes, use
fn yarn to make elongated French knots.
Work each knot over 2 sts at a slight angle
and wrap the yarn around the needle five
times. With bl yarn, make a stitch over the
center of the French knot. Using po yarn,
embroider a small nose in satin stitch. For
whiskers, cut 3in (8cm) strands of sewing
thread and thread through cheeks, then
trim. Sew ends of collar together and slide
over head onto neck.

Siamese

The superstars' choice, Vivian Leigh, Clark Gable, and James Dean all owned Siamese, as did Frank Zappa and Snoop Dogg. Chatty and friendly, Siamese cats are highly intelligent and trainable. Sometimes they have crossed eyes and a kink in their tails, and though these traits have mostly been bred out, ours do have crossed eyes. Siamese have a strong hold on the imagination of the 1950s child, due to Tao, the plucky Siamese in *The Incredible Journey*, and Si and Am, the terrifyingly sinister Siamese twins in *Lady and the Tramp*. Growing up, we had a Siamese called Tutu.

Siamese

The Siamese is a very elegant cat, simple and fairly quick to knit with only two colors. We have made twins.

Measurements
Length: 5½in (14cm)
Height to top of head: 5¼in (13cm)

Materials
- Pair of US 2 (2¾mm) knitting needles
- 4 spare US 2 (2¾mm) knitting needles or small stitch holders or safety pins
- Pair of US 2 (2¾mm) double-pointed knitting needles
- ⅛oz (5g) of Rowan Cashsoft 4ply in Bark 432 (bk)
- 1⅛oz (25g) of Rowan Cashsoft 4ply in Elite 451 (el)
- Tiny amount of Rowan Cashsoft 4ply in Cherish 453 (ch) for eyes
- Tiny amount of Rowan Pure Wool 4ply in Black 404 (bl) for pupils
- 2 pipecleaners
- Black sewing thread for whiskers
- Ribbon for neck

Abbreviations
See page 141.
See page 141 for Wrap Method.
See page 141 for Intarsia Technique.

Right Back Leg
With US 2 (2¾mm) needles and bk, cast on 7 sts.
Beg with a k row, work 2 rows st st.
Row 3: Inc, k2tog, k1, k2tog, inc. *(7 sts)*
Row 4: Purl.
Rep last 2 rows twice more.
Change to el.
Row 9: Knit.
Row 10 and every alt row: Purl.
Row 11: Inc, k5, inc. *(9 sts)*
Row 13: K2tog, k1, inc, k1, inc, k1, k2tog. *(9 sts)*
Row 15: K3, inc, k1, inc, k3. *(11 sts)*
Row 17: K2tog, k2, inc, k1, inc, k2, k2tog. *(11 sts)*
Row 19: K4, inc, k1, inc, k4. *(13 sts)*
Row 21: K5, inc, k1, inc, k5. *(15 sts)*
Row 23: K6, inc, k1, inc, k6. *(17 sts)*
Row 25: K7, inc, k1, inc, k7. *(19 sts)*
Row 26: Purl.*
Row 27: Bind off 9 sts, k to end (hold 10 sts on spare needle for Right Side of Body).

Left Back Leg
Work as for Right Back Leg to *.
Row 27: K10, bind off 9 sts (hold 10 sts on spare needle for Left Side of Body).

Right Front Leg
With US 2 (2¾mm) needles and bk, cast on 7 sts.
Beg with a k row, work 2 rows st st.
Row 3: Inc, k2tog, k1, k2tog, inc. *(7 sts)*
Row 4: Purl.
Rep last 2 rows once more.
Work 2 rows st st.
Change to el.
Row 9: Knit.
Row 10: Purl.
Work 4 rows st st.
Row 15: Inc, k5, inc. *(9 sts)*
Row 16: Purl.
Row 17: K3, inc, k1, inc, k3. *(11 sts)*

Row 18: Purl.
Row 19: K4, inc, k1, inc, k4. *(13 sts)*
Row 20: Purl.
Row 21: K5, inc, k1, inc, k5. *(15 sts)*
Row 22: Purl.**
Row 23: Bind off 7 sts, k to end (hold 8 sts on spare needle for Right Side of Body).

Left Front Leg
Work as for Right Front Leg to **.
Row 23: K8, bind off 7 sts (hold 8 sts on spare needle for Left Side of Body).

Right Side of Body
Row 1: With US 2 (2¾mm) needles and el, cast on 1 st, with RS facing k8 from spare needle of Right Front Leg. *(9 sts)*
Row 2: Purl.
Row 3: Inc, k8, cast on 8 sts. *(18 sts)*
Row 4: Purl.
Row 5: K18, cast on 6 sts. *(24 sts)*
Row 6: Purl.
Row 7: K24, with RS facing k10 from spare needle of Right Back Leg. *(34 sts)*
Beg with a p row, work 5 rows st st.
Row 13: K2tog, k32. *(33 sts)*
Row 14: P2tog, p31. *(32 sts)*
Work 3 rows st st.
Row 18: P2tog, p30. *(31 sts)*
Row 19: Knit.
Row 20: P2tog, p29. *(30 sts)*
Row 21: Knit.
Row 22: P3 (hold these 3 sts on spare needle for Tail), bind off 18 sts (hold rem 9 sts on spare needle for Neck).

Left Side of Body
Row 1: With US 2 (2¾mm) needles and el, cast on 1 st, with WS facing p8 from spare needle of Left Front Leg. *(9 sts)*
Row 2: Knit.
Row 3: Inc, p8, cast on 8 sts. *(18 sts)*
Row 4: Knit.
Row 5: P18, cast on 6 sts. *(24 sts)*

Head

The Siamese has a delicate, triangular-shaped head, which we have accentuated with a simple ribbon collar.

Row 6: Knit.

Row 7: P24, with WS facing p10 from spare needle of Left Back Leg. *(34 sts)*

Beg with a k row, work 5 rows st st.

Row 13: P2tog, p32. *(33 sts)*

Row 14: K2tog, k31. *(32 sts)*

Work 3 rows st st.

Row 18: K2tog, k30. *(31 sts)*

Row 19: Purl.

Row 20: K2tog, k29. *(30 sts)*

Row 21: Purl.

Row 22: K3 (hold these 3 sts on spare needle for Tail), bind off 18 sts (hold rem 9 sts on spare needle for Neck).

Neck and Head

Row 1: With US 2 (2¾mm) needles and el and RS facing, k9 from spare needle of Right Side of Body, then k9 from spare needle of Left Side of Body. *(18 sts)*

Row 2: P8, p2tog, p8. *(17 sts)*

Row 3: K4, k2tog, k5, k2tog, k4. *(15 sts)*

Row 4: P5, p2tog, p1, p2tog, p5. *(13 sts)*

Work 2 rows st st.

Row 7: K11, wrap and turn.

Row 8: P9, w&t.

Row 9: K9, w&t.

Row 10: P9, w&t.

Row 11: Knit to end. *(13 sts in total)*

Join in bk.

Row 12: Incel, p4el, p3bk, p4el, incel. *(15 sts)*

Row 13: K6el, k3bk, k6el.

Row 14: P3el, p2togel, p5bk, p2togel, p3el. *(13 sts)*

Row 15: K1el, k2togel, k7bk, k2togel, k1el. *(11 sts)*

Row 16: P2el, p7bk, p2el.

Row 17: K1el, k2togbk, k5bk, k2togbk, k1el. *(9 sts)*

Row 18: P1el, k2togbk, p3bk, p2togbk, p1el. *(7 sts)*

Cont in bk.

Row 19: K2tog, k3, k2tog. *(5 sts)*

Tail

With the use of a pipecleaner, you can give your Siamese a kink in his tail if you want.

Row 20: P2tog, p1, p2tog. *(3 sts)*
Row 21: K3tog and fasten off.

Tummy

With US 2 (2¾mm) needles and el, cast on 6 sts.
Beg with a k row, work 90 rows st st.
Change to bk.
Row 91: K2tog, k2, k2tog. *(4 sts)*
Row 92: Purl.
Work 2 rows st st.
Row 95: [K2tog] twice. *(2 sts)*
Row 96: P2tog and fasten off.

Ear

(make 2 the same)
With US 2 (2¾mm) needles and bk, cast on 7 sts.
Beg with a k row, work 4 rows st st.
Row 5: K2tog, k3, k2tog. *(5 sts)*
Row 6: Purl.
Row 7: K2tog, k1, k2tog. *(3 sts)*
Row 8: Purl.
Row 9: K3tog and fasten off.

Tail

With US 2 (2¾mm) double-pointed needles and bk and RS facing, k3 from spare needle of Right Side of Body for Tail, then k3 from spare needle of Left Side of Body for Tail. *(6 sts)*
Work in i-cord as follows:
Knit 10 rows.
Row 11: K2, k2tog, k2. *(5 sts)*
Knit 12 rows.
Row 24: K2tog, k1, k2tog. *(3 sts)*
Row 25: K3tog and fasten off.

To Finish

Sew in ends, leaving ends from bound off rows for sewing up. Using mattress or whip stitch, sew up legs starting at paw. Using mattress or whip stitch, sew along back of cat and down bottom. Using mattress or whip stitch, sew cast on row of tummy to bottom end of cat and sew final row to nose. Ease and sew tummy to fit body. Leave a 1in (2.5cm) gap between front and back legs on one side. Roll the pipecleaners in a small amount of stuffing and bend each one into a U shape. Fold over the ends (so they don't poke out of the paws) and slip into body, one pipecleaner down front legs and one down back legs. Stuff, and sew up gap with mattress stitch. Mold into shape. Sew ears to head, leaving about 3 sts between the two ears. For the eyes, use ch yarn to make elongated French knots. Work each knot over 2 sts at a slight angle and wrap the yarn around the needle five times. With bl yarn, make a stitch at bottom end to create a squint. Using bl yarn, embroider a small nose in satin stitch. For whiskers, cut 2in (5cm) strands of sewing thread and thread through cheeks, then trim. Cut ribbon to fit around neck and stitch in place.

Siamese Cat Sitting

The sitting Siamese has a characteristically enquiring expression.

Measurements
Length: 5½in (14cm)
Height to top of head: 5¼in (13cm)

Materials
- Pair of US 2 (2¾mm) knitting needles
- 2 spare US 2 (2¾mm) knitting needles or small stitch holders or safety pins
- Pair of US 2 (2¾mm) double-pointed knitting needles
- ⅛oz (5g) of Rowan Cashsoft 4ply in Bark 432 (bk)
- 1⅛oz (25g) of Rowan Cashsoft 4ply in Elite 451 (el)
- Tiny amount of Rowan Cashsoft 4ply in Cherish 453 (ch) for eyes
- Tiny amount of Rowan Pure Wool 4ply in Black 404 (bl) for pupils
- 2 pipecleaners
- Black sewing thread for whiskers
- Ribbon for neck

Abbreviations
See page 141.
See page 141 for Wrap Method.
See page 141 for Intarsia Technique.

Back Leg
(make 2 the same)
With US 2 (2¾mm) needles and bk, cast on 7 sts.
Beg with a k row, work 10 rows st st.
Change to el.
Row 11: K1, inc into next 5 sts, k1. *(12 sts)*
Row 12: Purl.
Row 13: K1, inc into next 3 sts, k4, inc into next 3 sts, k1. *(18 sts)*
Row 14: Purl.
Row 15: K6, inc into next 2 sts, k2, inc into next 2 sts, k6. *(22 sts)*
Row 16: Purl.
Row 17: K8, inc into next 2 sts, k2, inc into next 2 sts, k8. *(26 sts)*
Work 5 rows st st.
Row 23: K2tog, k22, k2tog. *(24 sts)*
Row 24: Purl.
Row 25: [K2tog] twice, k16, [k2tog] twice. *(20 sts)*
Row 26: P2tog, p16, p2tog. *(18 sts)*
Row 27: [K2tog] twice, k10, [k2tog] twice. *(14 sts)*
Row 28: Purl.
Row 29: K2tog, k10, k2tog. *(12 sts)*
Row 30: Purl.
Row 31: K2tog, k8, k2tog. *(10 sts)*
Row 32: Purl.
Bind off.

Right Front Leg
With US 2 (2¾mm) needles and bk, cast on 7 sts.
Beg with a k row, work 2 rows st st.
Row 3: Inc, k2tog, k1, k2tog, inc. *(7 sts)*
Row 4: Purl.
Rep last 2 rows once more.
Work 2 rows st st.
Change to el.
Row 9: Knit.
Row 10: Purl.
Work 4 rows st st.
Row 15: Inc, k5, inc. *(9 sts)*
Row 16: Purl.
Row 17: K3, inc, k1, inc, k3. *(11 sts)*
Row 18: Purl.
Row 19: K4, inc, k1, inc, k4. *(13 sts)*
Row 20: Purl.
Row 21: K5, inc, k1, inc, k5. *(15 sts)*
Row 22: Purl.
Row 23: K6, inc, k1, inc, k6. *(17 sts)*
Row 24: Purl.*
Row 25: Bind off 9 sts, k to end (hold 8 sts on spare needle for Right Side of Body).

Left Front Leg
Work as for Right Front Leg to *.
Row 25: K8, bind off 9 sts (hold 8 sts on spare needle for Left Side of Body).

Right Side of Body
With US 2 (2¾mm) needles and el, cast on 5 sts.
Beg with a k row, work 4 rows st st.
Row 5: Inc, k4. *(6 sts)*
Row 6: Purl.
Row 7: Inc, k5. *(7 sts)*
Row 8: Purl.
Row 9: Inc, k6. *(8 sts)*
Row 10: Purl.
Row 11: Inc, k7. *(9 sts)*
Row 12: Purl.
Row 13: Inc, k8. *(10 sts)*
Row 14: Purl.
Row 15: Inc, k9. *(11 sts)*
Row 16: Purl.
Row 17: Inc, k10. *(12 sts)*
Row 18: Purl.
Row 19: Inc, k11. *(13 sts)*
Row 20: Purl.
Row 21: Inc, k12. *(14 sts)*
Row 22: Purl.
Row 23: Inc, k13. *(15 sts)*
Row 24: P15, with WS facing p8 from spare needle for Right Front Leg, cast on 1 st. *(24 sts)*
Work 3 rows st st.
Row 28: P2tog, p22. *(23 sts)*
Row 29: Knit.
Row 30: P2tog, p21. *(22 sts)*
Row 31: Inc, k21. *(23 sts)*

Row 32: P2tog, p21. *(22 sts)*
Row 33: K20, k2tog. *(21 sts)*
Row 34: P2tog, p19. *(20 sts)*
Row 35: K18, k2tog. *(19 sts)*
Row 36: P2tog, p17. *(18 sts)*
Row 37: K16, k2tog. *(17 sts)*
Row 38: Bind off 2 sts, p to end. *(15 sts)*
Row 39: K2tog, k11, k2tog. *(13 sts)*
Row 40: Bind off 2 sts, k to end. *(11 sts)*
Row 41: K2tog, k7, k2tog. *(9 sts)*
Row 42: P2tog, p7 (hold 8 sts on spare needle for Neck).

Left Side of Body

With US 2 (2¾mm) needles and el, cast on 5 sts.
Beg with a p row, work 4 rows st st.
Row 5: Inc, p4. *(6 sts)*
Row 6: Knit.
Row 7: Inc, p5. *(7 sts)*
Row 8: Knit.
Row 9: Inc, p6. *(8 sts)*
Row 10: Knit.
Row 11: Inc, p7. *(9 sts)*
Row 12: Knit.
Row 13: Inc, p8. *(10 sts)*
Row 14: Knit.
Row 15: Inc, p9. *(11 sts)*
Row 16: Knit.
Row 17: Inc, p10. *(12 sts)*
Row 18: Knit.
Row 19: Inc, p11. *(13 sts)*
Row 20: Knit.
Row 21: Inc, p12. *(14 sts)*
Row 22: Knit.
Row 23: Inc, p13. *(15 sts)*
Row 24: K15, with RS facing k8 from spare needle for Left Front Leg, cast on 1 st.
(24 sts)
Work 3 rows st st.
Row 28: K2tog, k22. *(23 sts)*
Row 29: Purl.
Row 30: K2tog, k21. *(22 sts)*
Row 31: Inc, p21. *(23 sts)*

Row 32: K2tog, k21. *(22 sts)*
Row 33: P20, p2tog. *(21 sts)*
Row 34: K2tog, k19. *(20 sts)*
Row 35: P18, p2tog. *(19 sts)*
Row 36: K2tog, k17. *(18 sts)*
Row 37: P16, p2tog. *(17 sts)*
Row 38: Bind off 2 sts, k to end. *(15 sts)*
Row 39: P2tog, p11, p2tog. *(13 sts)*
Row 40: Bind off 2 sts, k to end. *(11 sts)*
Row 41: P2tog, p7, p2tog. *(9 sts)*
Row 42: K2tog, k7 (hold 8 sts on spare needle for Neck).

Neck and Head

Row 1: With US 2 (2¾mm) needles and el and RS facing, k8 from spare needle of Right Side of Body, then k8 from spare needle of Left Side of Body. *(16 sts)*
Row 2: P7, p2tog, p7. *(15 sts)*
Row 3: K4, k2tog, k3, k2tog, k4. *(13 sts)*
Row 4: Purl.
Work 2 rows st st.
Row 7: K11, wrap and turn.
Row 8: P9, w&t.
Row 9: K9, w&t.
Row 10: P9, w&t.
Row 11: Knit to end. *(13 sts in total)*
Join in bk.
Row 12: Incel, p4el, p3bk, p4el, incel. *(15 sts)*
Row 13: K6el, k3bk, k6el.
Row 14: P3el, p2togel, p5bk, p2togel, p3el. *(13 sts)*
Row 15: K1el, k2togel, k7bk, k2togel, k1el. *(11 sts)*
Row 16: P2el, p7bk, p2el.
Row 17: K1el, k2togbk, k5bk, k2togbk, k1el. *(9 sts)*
Row 18: P1el, p2togbk, p3bk, p2togbk, p1el. *(7 sts)*
Cont in bk.
Row 19: K2tog, k3, k2tog. *(5 sts)*
Row 20: P2tog, p1, p2tog. *(3 sts)*
Row 21: K3tog and fasten off.

Tummy

With US 2 (2¾mm) needles and el, cast on 6 sts.
Work 88 rows st st.
Change to bk.
Row 89: K2tog, k2, k2tog. *(4 sts)*
Row 90: Purl.
Row 91: [K2tog] twice. *(2 sts)*
Row 92: P2tog and fasten off.

Ear

(make 2 the same)
With US 2 (2¾mm) needles and bk, cast on 7 sts.
Beg with a k row, work 4 rows st st.
Row 5: K2tog, k3, k2tog. *(5 sts)*
Row 6: Purl.
Row 7: K2tog, k1, k2tog. *(3 sts)*
Row 8: Purl.
Row 9: K3tog and fasten off.

Tail

With US 2 (2¾mm) double-pointed needles and bk, cast on 6 sts.
Work in i-cord as follows:
Knit 10 rows.
Row 11: K2, k2tog, k2. *(5 sts)*
Knit 12 rows.
Row 24: K2tog, k1, k2tog. *(3 sts)*
Row 25: K3tog and fasten off.

To Finish

Sew in ends, leaving ends from bound off rows for sewing up. Using mattress or whip stitch, sew up legs starting at paw. Cut a pipecleaner to fit length of back leg, fold over the ends (so they don't poke out of the paws), and slip into leg. Lightly stuff and sew along top of back legs, then bend into shape as shown in photograph. Using mattress or whip stitch, sew along back of cat. Then, using mattress or whip stitch, sew cast on row of tummy to bottom end of cat and sew final row to nose. Ease and sew tummy to fit body. Leave a 1in (2.5cm) gap on one side. Roll a pipecleaner in a small amount of stuffing and bend into a U shape. Fold over the ends (so they don't poke out of the paws) and slip into body down front legs. Stuff, and sew up gap with mattress stitch. Using whip stitch, attach back legs to body, sewing along top of leg and down back edge as shown in photograph. To hold the legs in place, at about ½in (1cm) down from top of leg, sew the inside of the leg to the body. Mold into shape. Attach the tail, which can be positioned curled up or to the side. Sew ears to head, leaving about 3 sts between the two ears. For the eyes, use ch yarn to make elongated French knots. Work each knot over 2 sts at a slight angle and wrap the yarn around the needle five times. With bl yarn, make a stitch at bottom end to create a squint. For whiskers, cut 2in (5cm) strands of sewing thread and thread through cheeks, then trim. Cut ribbon to fit around neck and stitch in place.

Street

Orange

Pure orange-colored cats are generally male. Winston Churchill was so devoted to his cat, Jock, that his will stipulated that there should always be an orange cat in residence at his home, Chartwell. Orlando was the eponymous hero of Katherine Hale's beautifully illustrated children's books, while Audrey Hepburn's cat in *Breakfast at Tiffany's* was called Orangey. Jones, an orange cat, has a small but vital role in the *Alien* movies.

Orange

This is one of the more complex cats. For an easier version, you can reduce the number of stripes or knit him in just orange-colored yarn.

Measurements

Length: 6in (15cm)
Height to top of head: 6in (15cm)

Materials

- Pair of US 2 (2¾mm) knitting needles
- 2 spare US 2 (2¾mm) knitting needles or small stitch holders or safety pins
- Pair of US 2 (2¾mm) double-pointed knitting needles
- Tiny amount of Rowan Pure Wool 4ply in Snow 412 (sn)
- ½oz (15g) of Rowan Felted Tweed in Gilt 160 (gt)
- ¼oz (10g) of Rowan Kidsilk Haze in Ember 644 (em)
- NOTE: Use gt and em yarns held together to make yarn A
- ½oz (15g) of Rowan Pure Wool 4ply in Quarry Tile 457 (qt)
- ¼oz (10g) of Rowan Kidsilk Haze in Brick 649 (br)
- NOTE: Use qt and br yarns held together to make yarn B
- Small amount of Rowan Cashsoft 4ply in Fennel 436 (fn) for eyes and collar
- Tiny amount of Rowan Pure Wool 4ply in Black 404 (bl) for pupils
- Cream sewing thread for whiskers
- Two pipecleaners
- Bell for collar (optional)

Abbreviations

See page 141.
See page 141 for Wrap Method.
See page 141 for Stranding or Fair Isle Technique.

Left Back Leg

With US 2 (2¾mm) needles and sn, cast on 9 sts.
Beg with a k row, work 3 rows st st.
Cont in A and B.
Row 4: P5A, p4B.
Row 5: K3A, k3B, k3A.
Row 6: P2A, p1B, p6A.
Row 7: K4B, k3A, k2B.
Row 8: P3A, p3B, p3A.
Row 9: K4A, k4B, k1A.
Row 10: P4B, p5A.**
Row 11: K1B, incB into next 2 sts, k3A, incA into next 2 sts, k1B. *(13 sts)*
Row 12: P2B, p6A, p2B, p3A.
Row 13: K1A, incA into next 4 sts, k3B, incA into next 4 sts, k1A. *(21 sts)*
Row 14: P8A, p3B, p7A, p3B.
Row 15: K7B, incA into next 2 sts, k3A, incA into next 2 sts, k7A. *(25 sts)*
Row 16: P17A, p3B, p5A.
Row 17: K7A, k2B, incB into next 2 sts, k3A, incA into next 2 sts, k9A. *(29 sts)*
Row 18: P14A, p3B, p12A.
Row 19: K15A, k3B, k11A.
Row 20: P22A, p7B.
Row 21: K3A, k6B, k20A.
Row 22: P18A, p5B, p6A.
Row 23: [K2togA] 3 times, k3A, k4B, k10A, [k2togA] 3 times. *(23 sts)*
Row 24: P11A, p2B, p10A.
Row 25: [K2togB] twice, k2B, k13A, [k2togA] twice. *(19 sts)*
Row 26: P13A, p4B, p2A.
Row 27: [K2togA] twice, k4B, k7A, [k2togA] twice. *(15 sts)*
Row 28: [P2togA] twice, p4A, p3B, [p2togA] twice. *(11 sts)*
Bind off.

Right Back Leg

Work as for Left Back Leg to **.
Row 11: K1B, incA into next 2 sts, k3A, incB into next 2 sts, k1B. *(13 sts)*
Row 12: P3A, p2B, p6A, p2B.
Row 13: K1A, incA into next 4 sts, k3B, incB into next 4 sts, k1A. *(21 sts)*
Row 14: P3B, p7A, p3B, P8A.
Row 15: K7A, incA into next 2 sts, k3A, incA into next 2 sts, k7B. *(25 sts)*
Row 16: P5A, p3B, p17A.
Row 17: K9A, incA into next 2 sts, k3A, incB into next 2 sts, k2B, k7A. *(29 sts)*
Row 18: P12A, p3B, p14A.
Row 19: K11A, k3B, k15A.
Row 20: P7B, p22A.
Row 21: K20A, k6B, k3A.
Row 22: P6A, p5B, p18A.
Row 23: [K2togA] 3 times, k10A, k4B, k3A, [k2togA] 3 times. *(23 sts)*
Row 24: P10A, p2B, p11A.
Row 25: [K2togA] twice, k13A, K2B, [k2togB] twice. *(19 sts)*
Row 26: P2A, p4B, p13A.
Row 27: [K2togA], k7A, k4B, [k2togA] twice. *(15 sts)*
Row 28: [P2togA] twice, p3B, p4A, [p2togA] twice. *(11 sts)*
Bind off.

Right Front Leg

With US 2 (2¾mm) needles and A, cast on 7 sts.
Beg with a k row, work 2 rows st st.
Row 3: Inc, k2tog, k1, k2tog, inc. *(7 sts)*
Join in B.
Row 4: P2A, p3B, p2A.
Row 5: IncA, k2togA, k1A, k2togB, incB. *(7 sts)*

Row 6: P2B, p5A.
Row 7: K7A.
Row 8: P2A, p5B.
Row 9: K3B, k4A.
Row 10: P5A, p2B.
Row 11: K7A.
Row 12: P4B, p3A.
Row 13: IncA, k1A, k4B, incB. *(9 sts)*
Row 14: P2B, p7A.
Row 15: K4A, k3B, k2A.
Row 16: P5A, p3B, p1A.
Row 17: IncB, k6B, k1A, incA. *(11 sts)*
Row 18: P7A, p4B.*
Row 19: Bind off 5 sts, k to end (hold 6 sts on spare needle for Right Front Leg).

Left Front Leg
Work as for Right Front Leg to *.
Row 19: K6 sts, bind off 5 sts (hold 6 sts on spare needle for Left Front Leg).

Right Side of Body
With US 2 (2¾mm) needles, cast on 2 sts B and 2 sts A.
Row 1: K2A, k2B.
Row 2: P2B, p2A.
Row 3: IncA, k1A, k2B. *(5 sts)*
Row 4: P2B, p3A.
Row 5: IncA, k1A, k2B, incB. *(7 sts)*
Row 6: P3B, p4A.
Row 7: IncA, k4A, k2B. *(8 sts)*
Row 8: P1B, p2A, p3B, p2A.
Row 9: IncA, k7B. *(9 sts)*
Row 10: P3B, p2A, p3B, p1A.
Row 11: IncA, k1B, k5A, k2B. *(10 sts)*
Row 12: P1B, p9A.
Row 13: IncA, k2A, k7B. *(11 sts)*
Row 14: P8B, p3A.
Row 15: IncA, k3B, k3A, k4B. *(12 sts)*
Row 16: P3B, p6A, p2B, p1A, p6A from spare needle of Right Front Leg, cast on 2 sts A. *(20 sts)*
Row 17: K4A, k3B, k2A, k1B, k8A, k2B.
Row 18: P1B, p11A, p2B, p4A, p1B, p1A.

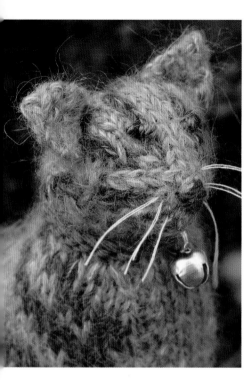

Face

Move the ears or change the color of the eyes to match your own orange cat.

Row 19: IncA, k1A, k1B, k4A, k2B, k10A, k1B. *(21 sts)*
Row 20: P2B, p3A, p7B, p4A, p2B, p3A.
Row 21: IncA, k3A, k2B, k6A, k5B, k1A, k3B. *(22 sts)*
Row 22: P6B, p8A, p3B, p3A, p1B, p1A.
Row 23: K2A, k1B, k3A, k3B, k8A, k5B.
Row 24: P2togB, p2B, p2A, p10B, p2A, p2B, p2A. *(21 sts)*
Row 25: K2A, k3B, k2A, k10B, k2A, k2B.
Row 26: P2togB, p2A, p2B, p3A, p2B, p4A, p5B, p1A. *(20 sts)*
Row 27: K1A, k2B, k1A, k3B, k4A, k2B, k3A, k2B, k1A, k1B.
Row 28: P2togB, p1B, p3A, p2B, p4A, p3B, p1A, p2B, p2A. *(19 sts)*
Row 29: K3A, k2B, k1A, k3B, k3A, k3B, k2A, k2B.
Row 30: P2togB, p1A, p3B, p4A, p2B, p2A, p1B, p4A. *(18 sts)*
Row 31: K2togA, k2A, k2B, k2A, k2B, k4A, k2B, k2togB. *(16 sts)*
Row 32: Bind off 3 sts B and 2 sts A, p9A ibos, p2togA (hold 10 sts on spare needle for Neck).

Left Side of Body

With US 2 (2¾mm) needles, cast on 2 sts B and 2 sts A.
Row 1: P2A, p2B.
Row 2: K2B, k2A.
Row 3: IncA, p1A, p2B. *(5 sts)*
Row 4: K2B, k3A.
Row 5: IncA, p1A, p2B, incB. *(7 sts)*
Row 6: K3B, k4A.
Row 7: IncA, p4A, p2B. *(8 sts)*
Row 8: K1B, k2A, k3B, k2A.
Row 9: IncA, p7B. *(9 sts)*
Row 10: K3B, k2A, k3B, k1A.
Row 11: IncA, p1B, p5A, p2B. *(10 sts)*
Row 12: K1B, k9A.
Row 13: IncA, p2A, p7B. *(11 sts)*
Row 14: K8B, k3A.
Row 15: IncA, p3B, p3A, p4B. *(12 sts)*

Row 16: K3B, k6A, k2B, k1A, k6A from spare needle of Left Front Leg, cast on 2 sts A. *(20 sts)*
Row 17: P4A, p3B, p2A, p1B, p8A, p2B.
Row 18: K1B, k11A, k2B, k4A, k1B, k1A.
Row 19: IncA, p1A, p1B, p4A, p2B, p10A, p1B. *(21 sts)*
Row 20: K2B, k3A, k7B, k4A, k2B, k3A.
Row 21: IncA, p3A, p2B, p6A, p5B, p1A, p3B. *(22 sts)*
Row 22: K6B, k8A, k3B, k3A, k1B, k1A.
Row 23: P2A, p1B, p3A, p3B, p8A, p5B.
Row 24: K2togB, k2B, k2A, k10B, k2A, k2B, k2A. *(21 sts)*
Row 25: P2A, p3B, p2A, p10B, p2A, p2B.
Row 26: K2togB, k2A, k2B, k3A, k2B, k4A, k5B, k1A. *(20 sts)*
Row 27: P1A, p2B, p1A, p3B, p4A, p2B, p3A, p2B, p1A, p1B.
Row 28: K2togB, k1B, k3A, k2B, k4A, k3B, k1A, k2B, k2A. *(19 sts)*
Row 29: P3A, p2B, p1A, p3B, p3A, p3B, p2A, p2B.
Row 30: K2togB, k1A, k3B, k4A, k2B, k2A, k1B, k4A. *(18 sts)*
Row 31: P2togA, p2A, p2B, p2A, p2B, p4A, p2B, p2togB. *(16 sts)*
Row 32: Bind off 3 sts B and 2 sts A, k9A ibos, k2togA (hold 10 sts on spare needle for Neck).

Neck and Head

Row 1: With US 2 (2¾mm) needles and RS facing, k4A, k2togB, k1B, k3A from spare needle of Right Side of Body, then k3A, k1B, k2togB, k4A from spare needle of Left Side of Body. *(18 sts)*
Row 2: P2A, p1B, p2togA, p2B, p4A, p2B, p2togA, p1B, p2A. *(16 sts)*
Row 3: K2A, k1B, k1A, k2togB, k1B, k2A, k1B, k2togB, k1A, k1B, k2A. *(14 sts)*
Row 4: P3A, p1B, incA, p1B, p2A, p1B, incA, p1B, p3A. *(16 sts)*

Row 5: K3A, k1B, k2A, k1B, k2A, k1B, k2A, k1B, k1A, wrap and turn.
Row 6: P1A, p1B, p2A, p1B, p2A, p1B, p2A, p1B, p1A, w&t.
Row 7: K1A, k1B, k2A, k1B, k2A, k1B, k2A, k1B, k1A, w&t.
Row 8: P1B, p2A, p1B, p4A, p1B, p2A, p1B, w&t.
Row 9: K1B, k2A, k1B, k4A, k1B, k2A, k1B, w&t.
Row 10: P1B, p2A, p1B, p4A, p1B, p2A, p1B, w&t.
Row 11: K1B, k1A, k1B, k2A, k2B, k2A, k1B, k1A, k1B, k2A. *(16 sts on right-hand needle)*
Row 12: P1A, p1B, p2A, p1B, p2A, p2B, p2A, p1B, p2A, p1B, p1A.
Row 13: K1A, k1B, k2A, k1B, k2A, k2B, k2A, k1B, k1A, wrap and turn.
Row 14: P1A, p1B, p2A, p2B, p2A, p1B, p1A, w&t.
Row 15: K1B, k2A, k1B, k2A, k1B, k2A, k1B, w&t.
Row 16: P1B, p2A, p1B, p2A, p1B, p2A, p1B, w&t.
Rep last 2 rows once more.
Row 19: K1A, k1B, k1A, k1B, k2A, k1B, k1A, k1B, k2A, k1B, k1A. *(16 sts on right-hand needle)*
Row 20: P1A, p1B, [p2togA] twice, p1B, p2A, p1B, [p2togA] twice, p1B, p1A. *(12 sts)*
Row 21: K3A, k2togB, k2A, k2togB, k3A. *(10 sts)*
Cont in A.
Row 22: P2, p2tog, p2, p2tog, p2. *(8 sts)*
Row 23: [K2tog] 4 times. *(4 sts)*
Bind off.

Tummy

With US 2 (2¾mm) needles and A, cast on 5 sts.
Beg with a k row, work 6 rows st st.
Row 7: Inc, k3, inc. *(7 sts)*
Work 17 rows st st.
Row 25: K2tog, k3, k2tog. *(5 sts)*

Work 33 rows st st.
Row 59: K2tog, k1, k2tog. *(3 sts)*
Work 4 rows st st.
Row 64: P3tog and fasten off.

Ear

(make 2 the same)
With US 2 (2¾mm) needles and A, cast on 6 sts.
Beg with a k row, work 2 rows st st.
Row 3: K2tog, k2, k2tog. *(4 sts)*
Row 4: Purl.
Row 5: [K2tog] twice. *(2 sts)*
Row 6: P2tog and fasten off.

Tail

With US 2 (2¾mm) double-pointed needles and B, cast on 6 sts.
Work in i-cord as follows:
Knit 4 rows.
Join in A.
Row 5: K1A, k4B, k1A.
Row 6: K2A, k2B, k2A.
Row 7: K6A.
Row 8: K2A, k2B, k2A.
Row 9: K1A, k4B, k1A.
Knit 2 rows in B.
Rep rows 5–11 three times more.
Cont in A.
Row 33: K2tog, k2, k2tog. *(4 sts)*
Knit 2 rows.
Row 36: [K2tog] twice. *(2 sts)*
Row 37: K2tog and fasten off.

Collar

With US 2 (2¾mm) needles and fn, cast on 26 sts.
Knit 1 row.
Bind off.

To Finish

Sew in ends, leaving ends from bound off rows for sewing up. Using mattress or whip stitch, sew up legs starting at paw. Cut a pipecleaner to fit length of back leg, fold over the ends (so they don't poke out of the paws), and slip into leg. Lightly stuff and sew along top of back legs, then bend into shape as shown in photograph. Using mattress or whip stitch, sew along back of cat. At head, fold in half and sew bound off edges of nose together. Using mattress or whip stitch, sew cast on row of tummy to bottom end of cat and sew final row to nose. Ease and sew tummy to fit body. Leave a 1in (2.5cm) gap on one side. Roll a pipecleaner in a small amount of stuffing and bend into a U shape. Fold over the ends (so they don't poke out of the paws) and slip into body down front legs. Stuff, and sew up gap with mattress stitch. Using whip stitch, attach back legs to body, sewing along top of leg and down back edge as shown in photograph. To hold the legs in place, at about ½in (1cm) down from top of leg, sew the inside of the leg to the body. Mold into shape. Attach the tail as in photograph. Sew ears to head, leaving about 3 sts between the two ears. With qt yarn, embroider a small nose in satin stitch. For the eyes, use fn yarn to make elongated French knots. Work each knot over 2 sts at a slight angle and wrap the yarn around the needle five times. With bl yarn, make a stitch over the center of the French knot. For whiskers, cut 3in (8cm) strands of sewing thread and thread through cheeks, then trim. Slip optional bell onto collar, sew ends of collar together, then slide collar over head onto neck.

Black & White

This cat is a popular choice in the Downing Street residence of British Prime Ministers. Wilberforce, a champion mouser, was cat-in-residence with four Prime Ministers—Edward Heath, Harold Wilson, James Callaghan, and Margaret Thatcher. When he retired, he was replaced by Humphrey, who lived there with three Prime Ministers— Margaret Thatcher, John Major, and Tony Blair—before retiring in 1997 under slightly mysterious circumstances shortly after the arrival of Tony Blair.

Black & White

This is the classic black and white cat, but the coloring can be used for other cats.

Measurements

Length: 9in (23cm)
Height to top of head: 5¼in (13cm)

Materials

- Pair of US 2 (2¾mm) knitting needles
- 4 spare US 2 (2¾mm) knitting needles or small stitch holders or safety pins
- Pair of US 2 (2¾mm) double-pointed knitted needles
- ¼oz (10g) of Rowan Pure Wool 4ply in Snow 412 (sn)
- ½oz (15g) of Rowan Pure Wool 4ply in Black 404 (bl)
- Small amount of Rowan Pure Wool 4ply in Framboise 456 (fr) for collar
- Tiny amount of Rowan Pure Wool 4ply in Eau De Nil 450 (en) for eyes
- Tiny amount of Rowan Pure Wool 4ply in Powder 443 (po) for nose
- 2 pipecleaners
- White sewing thread for whiskers
- Bell for collar (optional)

Abbreviations

See page 141.
See page 141 for Wrap Method.
See page 141 for Intarsia Technique.

Right Back Leg

With US 2 (2¾mm) needles and sn, cast on 9 sts.
Work 2 rows st st.
Row 3: Inc, k1, k2tog, k1, k2tog, k1, inc. *(9 sts)*
Row 4: Purl.
Change to bl.
Rep last 2 rows once more.
Work 4 rows st st.
Row 11: Inc, k7, inc. *(11 sts)*
Row 12: Purl.
Row 13: K2tog, k1, inc, k3, inc, k1, k2tog. *(11 sts)*
Row 14: P2tog, p1, inc, p3, inc, p1, p2tog. *(11 sts)*
Row 15: K2tog, k1, inc, k1, inc, k1, inc, k1, k2tog. *(12 sts)*
Row 16: Purl.
Row 17: K3, inc, k4, inc, k3. *(14 sts)*
Row 18: Purl.
Row 19: K3, inc, k6, inc, k3. *(16 sts)*
Row 20: Purl.
Row 21: K3, inc, k8, inc, k3. *(18 sts)*
Row 22: Purl.
Row 23: Knit.*
Row 24: P10, bind off 8 sts (hold 10 sts on spare needle for Right Side of Body).

Left Back Leg

Work as for Right Back Leg to *.
Row 24: Bind off 8 sts, p to end (hold 10 sts on spare needle for Left Side of Body).

Right Front Leg

With US 2 (2¾mm) needles and sn, cast on 9 sts.
Work 2 rows st st.
Change to bl.
Row 3: Inc, k1, k2tog, k1, k2tog, k1, inc. *(9 sts)*
Row 4: Purl.
Rep last 2 rows once more.
Work 6 rows st st.
Row 13: Inc, k7, inc. *(11 sts)*
Work 3 rows st st.
Row 17: K3, inc, k3, inc, k3. *(13 sts)*
Row 18: Purl.
Row 19: K4, inc, k3, inc, k4. *(15 sts)*
Row 20: Purl.**
Row 21: Bind off 7 sts, k to end (hold 8 sts on spare needle for Right Side of Body).

Left Front Leg

Work as for Right Front Leg to **.
Row 21: K8, bind off 7 sts (hold 8 sts on spare needle for Left Side of Body).

Right Side of Body

Row 1: With US 2 (2¾mm) needles and bl, cast on 2 sts, with RS facing k8bl from spare needle of Right Front Leg, cast on 7 sts sn. *(17 sts)*
Row 2: P7sn, p10bl.
Row 3: Incbl, k9bl, k6sn, k1bl, cast on 6 sts bl, with RS facing k10bl from spare needle of Right Back Leg. *(34 sts)*
Row 4: P17bl, p6sn, p11bl.
Row 5: Incbl, k10bl, k6sn, k17bl. *(35 sts)*
Row 6: P17bl, p6sn, p12bl.
Row 7: K1sn, k11bl, k6sn, k17bl.
Row 8: P17bl, p5sn, p12bl, p1sn.
Row 9: Incsn, k1sn, k11bl, k4sn, k18bl. *(36 sts)*
Row 10: P18bl, p4sn, p11bl, p3sn.
Row 11: K3sn, k11bl, k3sn, k18bl, incbl. *(37 sts)*
Row 12: P20bl, p2sn, p11bl, p4sn.
Row 13: Incsn, k3sn, k21bl, incbl, k11bl. *(39 sts)*
Row 14: P34bl, p5sn.
Row 15: K5sn, k34bl.
Row 16: P2togbl, p31bl, p6sn. *(38 sts)*
Row 17: K6sn, k22bl, incbl, k7bl, k2togbl. *(38 sts)*
Row 18: P2togbl, p29bl, p7sn. *(37 sts)*

Row 19: K2togsn, k6sn, k27bl, k2togbl. *(35 sts)*

Row 20: Bind off 26 sts bl, p1bl ibos, p8sn (hold 9 sts on spare needle for Neck).

Left Side of Body

Row 1: With US 2 (2¾mm) needles and bl, cast on 2 sts, with WS facing p8bl from spare needle of Left Front Leg, cast on 7 sts sn. *(17 sts)*

Row 2: K7sn, k10bl.

Row 3: Incbl, p9bl, p6sn, p1bl, cast on 6 sts bl, with WS facing p10bl from spare needle of Left Back Leg. *(34 sts)*

Row 4: K17bl, k6sn, k11bl.

Row 5: Incbl, p10bl, p6sn, p17bl. *(35 sts)*

Row 6: K17bl, k6sn, k12bl.

Row 7: P1sn, p11bl, p6sn, p17bl.

Row 8: K17bl, k5sn, k12bl, k1sn.

Row 9: Incsn, p1sn, p11bl, p4sn, p18bl. *(36 sts)*

Row 10: K18bl, k4sn, k11bl, k3sn.

Row 11: P3sn, p11bl, p3sn, p18bl, incbl. *(37 sts)*

Row 12: K20bl, k2sn, k11bl, k4sn.

Row 13: Incsn, p3sn, p21bl, incbl, p11bl. *(39 sts)*

Row 14: K34bl, k5sn.

Row 15: P5sn, p34bl.

Row 16: K2togbl, k31bl, k6sn. *(38 sts)*

Row 17: P6sn, p22bl, incbl, p7bl, p2togbl. *(38 sts)*

Row 18: K2togbl, k29bl, k7sn. *(37 sts)*

Row 19: P2togsn, p6sn, p27bl, p2togbl. *(35 sts)*

Row 20: Bind off 26 sts bl, k1bl ibos, k8sn (hold 9 sts on spare needle for Neck).

Neck and Head

Row 1: With US 2 (2¾mm) needles and RS facing, k4sn, k2togsn, k1sn, k2bl from spare needle of Right Side of Body, then k2bl, k1sn, k2togsn, k4sn from spare needle of Left Side of Body. *(16 sts)*

Legs

After stuffing, bend the legs to the required shape and fold at the ankle to make a paw.

Row 2: P5sn, p6bl, p5sn.
Row 3: K2sn, incsn, k1sn, k8bl, k1sn, incsn, k2sn. *(18 sts)*
Row 4: P4sn, p10bl, p4sn.
Row 5: K4sn, k10bl, k1sn, wrap and turn.
Row 6: P1sn, p10bl, p1sn, w&t.
Row 7: K1sn, k10bl, k1sn, w&t.
Rep last 2 rows once more.
Row 10: P1sn, p10bl, p1sn, w&t.
Row 11: K1sn, k10bl, k4sn. *(18 sts)*
Row 12: P3sn, p12bl, p3sn.
Row 13: K3sn, k11bl, wrap and turn.
Row 14: P10bl, w&t.
Row 15: K10bl, w&t.
Row 16: P10bl, w&t.
Row 17: K11bl, k3sn. *(18 sts)*
Row 18: P2togsn, p1sn, p1bl, p2togbl, p2bl, p2togsn, p2bl, p2togbl, p1bl, p1sn, p2togsn. *(13 sts)*
Row 19: K3sn, k2togbl, k1bl, k1sn, k1bl, k2togbl, k3sn. *(11 sts)*
Cont in sn.
Row 20: P2, p2tog, p3, p2tog, p2. *(9 sts)*
Row 21: K9.
Row 22: P2, p2tog, p1, p2tog, p2. *(7 sts)*
Bind off.

Tummy

With US 2 (2¾mm) needles and bl, cast on 6 sts.
Work 2 rows st st.
Row 3: K2tog, k2, k2tog. *(4 sts)*
Row 4: [P2tog] twice. *(2 sts)*
Change to sn.
Work 8 rows st st.
Row 13: [Inc] twice. *(4 sts)*
Work 5 rows st st.
Row 19: Inc, k2, inc. *(6 sts)*
Work 17 rows st st.
Row 37: K2tog, k2, k2tog. *(4 sts)*
Row 38: [P2tog] twice. *(2 sts)*
Work 4 rows st st.
Row 43: [Inc] twice. *(4 sts)*
Row 44: Inc, p2, inc. *(6 sts)*

Work 7 rows st st.
Row 52: P2tog, p2, p2tog. *(4 sts)*
Work 20 rows st st.
Row 73: [K2tog] twice. *(2 sts)*
Work 2 rows st st.
Row 76: P2tog and fasten off.

Ear

(make 2 the same)
With US 2 (2¾mm) needles and bl, cast on 6 sts.
Work 2 rows st st.
Row 3: K2tog, k2, k2tog. *(4 sts)*
Row 4: Purl.
Row 5: [K2tog] twice. *(2 sts)*
Row 6: P2tog and fasten off.

Tail

With US 2 (2¾mm) double-pointed needles and bl, cast on 9 sts.
Work in i-cord as follows:
Knit 12 rows.
Row 13: K2tog, k5, k2tog. *(7 sts)*
Knit 12 rows.
Row 26: K2tog, k3, k2tog. *(5 sts)*
Knit 1 row.
Change to sn.
Knit 4 rows.
Row 32: K2tog, k1, k2tog. *(3 sts)*
Row 33: K3tog and fasten off.

Collar

With US 2 (2¾mm) needles and fr, cast on 26 sts.
Knit 1 row.
Bind off.

To Finish

Sew in ends, leaving ends from bound off rows for sewing up. Using mattress or whip stitch, sew up legs starting at paw. Using mattress or whip stitch, sew along back of cat and down bottom. At head, fold in half and sew bound off edges of nose together. Using mattress or whip stitch, sew cast on row of tummy to bottom end of cat and sew final row to nose. Ease and sew tummy to fit body, matching curves to legs. Leave a 1in (2.5cm) gap between front and back legs on one side. Roll the pipecleaners in a small amount of stuffing and bend each one into a U shape. Fold over the ends (so they don't poke out of the paws) and slip into body, one pipecleaner down front legs and one down back legs. Stuff, and sew up gap with mattress stitch. Mold into shape. Attach the tail as in photograph. Sew ears to head, leaving about 3 sts between the two ears. For the eyes, use en yarn to make elongated French knots. Work each knot over 2 sts at a slight angle and wrap the yarn around the needle five times. With bl yarn, make a stitch over the center of the French knot. Using po yarn, embroider a small nose in satin stitch. For whiskers, cut 3in (8cm) strands of sewing thread and thread through cheeks, then trim. Slip optional bell onto collar, sew ends of collar together, then slide collar over head onto neck.

Black & White Cat Sitting

For a smooth finish, use the intarsia method when knitting this cat.

Measurements

Length: 7in (18cm)
Height to top of head: 5¼in (13cm)

Materials

- Pair of US 2 (2¾mm) knitting needles
- 2 spare US 2 (2¾mm) knitting needles or small stitch holders or safety pins
- Pair of US 2 (2¾mm) double-pointed knitting needles
- ½oz (15g) of Rowan Pure Wool 4ply in Black 404 (bl)
- ¼oz (10g) of Rowan Pure Wool 4ply in Snow 412 (sn)
- Small amount of Rowan Pure Wool 4ply in Framboise 456 (fr)
- Tiny amount of Rowan Pure Wool 4ply in Eau De Nil 450 (en) for eyes
- Tiny amount of Rowan Pure Wool 4ply in Powder 443 (po) for nose
- 2 pipecleaners
- White sewing thread for whiskers
- Bell for collar (optional)

Abbreviations

See page 141.
See page 141 for Wrap Method.
See page 141 for Intarsia Technique.

Back Leg

(make 2 the same)
With US 2 (2¾mm) needles and sn, cast on 9 sts.
Beg with a k row, work 4 rows st st.
Change to bl.
Row 5: K2, k2tog, k1, k2tog, k2. *(7 sts)*
Work 5 rows st st.
Row 11: Inc into next 3 sts, k1, inc into next 3 sts. *(13 sts)*
Row 12: Purl.
Row 13: K2, inc into next 4 sts, k1, inc into next 4 sts, k2. *(21 sts)*
Row 14: Purl.
Row 15: K8, inc into next 2 sts, k1, inc into next 2 sts, k8. *(25 sts)*
Row 16: Purl.
Row 17: K10, inc into next 2 sts, k1, inc into next 2 sts, k10. *(29 sts)*
Row 18: Purl.
Row 19: K12, inc into next 2 sts, k1, inc into next 2 sts, k12. *(33 sts)*
Work 5 rows st st.
Row 25: K2tog, k12, k2tog, k1, k2tog, k12, k2tog. *(29 sts)*
Row 26: P2tog, p10, p2tog, p1, p2tog, p10, p2tog. *(25 sts)*
Row 27: K2tog, k8, k2tog, k1, k2tog, k8, k2tog. *(21 sts)*
Row 28: P2tog, p6, p2tog, p1, p2tog, p6, p2tog. *(17 sts)*
Bind off.

Right Front Leg

With US 2 (2¾mm) needles and sn, cast on 9 sts.
Beg with a k row, work 2 rows st st.
Row 3: Inc, k1, k2tog, k1, k2tog, k1, inc. *(9 sts)*
Row 4: Purl. Rep last 2 rows once more.
Work 6 rows st st.
Row 13: Inc, k7, inc. *(11 sts)*
Work 5 rows st st.*
Row 19: Bind off 5 sts, k to end (hold 6 sts on spare needle for Right Side of Body).

Left Front Leg

Work as for Right Front Leg to *.
Row 19: K6, bind off 5 sts (hold 6 sts on spare needle for Left Side of Body).

Right Side of Body

With US 2 (2¾mm) needles and bl, cast on 5 sts.
Beg with a k row, work 4 rows st st.
Row 5: Inc, k4. *(6 sts)*
Row 6: Purl.
Row 7: Inc, k5. *(7 sts)*
Row 8: P6, inc. *(8 sts)*
Row 9: Inc, k7. *(9 sts)*
Row 10: P8, inc. *(10 sts)*
Row 11: Inc, k9. *(11 sts)*
Row 12: P10, inc. *(12 sts)*
Join in sn.
Row 13: Incsn, k11bl. *(13 sts)*
Row 14: P11bl, p1sn, incsn. *(14 sts)*
Row 15: Incsn, k2sn, k11bl. *(15 sts)*
Row 16: P11bl, p3sn, p1bl, p6sn from spare needle of Right Front Leg, cast on 2 sts sn. *(23 sts)*
Row 17: K8sn, k2bl, k2sn, k11bl.
Row 18: P11bl, p2sn, p2bl, p7sn, incsn. *(24 sts)*
Row 19: K8sn, k3bl, k2sn, k11bl.
Row 20: P12bl, p1sn, p4bl, p7sn. *(24 sts)*
Row 21: K7sn, k17bl.
Row 22: P18bl, p5sn, incsn. *(25 sts)*
Row 23: K7sn, k18bl.
Row 24: P2togbl, p17bl, p6sn. *(24 sts)*
Row 25: K6sn, k18bl.
Row 26: P18bl, p5sn, incsn. *(25 sts)*
Row 27: K7sn, k18bl.
Row 28: P2togbl, p15bl, p8sn. *(24 sts)*
Row 29: K8sn, k16bl.
Row 30: P2togbl, p14bl, p8sn. *(23 sts)*
Row 31: K8sn, k13bl, k2togbl. *(22 sts)*
Row 32: P2togbl, p11bl, p9sn. *(21 sts)*
Row 33: K9sn, k10bl, k2togbl. *(20 sts)*
Row 34: P2togbl, p9bl, p9sn. *(19 sts)*
Row 35: K9sn, k8bl, k2togbl. *(18 sts)*

Body

Stuff the body well to exaggerate the curve of the cat's back.

Row 36: Bind off 7bl, p2bl ibos, p9sn (hold 11 sts on spare needle for Neck).

Left Side of Body

With US 2 (2¾mm) needles and bl, cast on 5 sts.

Beg with a p row, work 4 rows st st.

Row 5: Inc, p4. *(6 sts)*
Row 6: Knit.
Row 7: Inc, p5. *(7 sts)*
Row 8: K6, inc. *(8 sts)*
Row 9: Inc, p7. *(9 sts)*
Row 10: K8, inc. *(10 sts)*
Row 11: Inc, p9. *(11 sts)*
Row 12: K10, inc. *(12 sts)*
Join in sn.
Row 13: Incsn, p11bl. *(13 sts)*
Row 14: K11bl, k1sn, incsn. *(14 sts)*
Row 15: Incsn, p2sn, p11bl. *(15 sts)*
Row 16: K11bl, k3sn, k1bl, k6sn from spare needle of Left Front Leg, cast on 2 sts sn. *(23 sts)*
Row 17: P8sn, p2bl, p2sn, p11bl.
Row 18: K11bl, k2sn, k2bl, k7sn, incsn. *(24 sts)*
Row 19: P8sn, p3bl, p2sn, p11bl.
Row 20: K12bl, k1sn, k4bl, k7sn. *(24 sts)*
Row 21: P7sn, p17bl.
Row 22: K18bl, k5sn, incsn. *(25 sts)*
Row 23: P7sn, p18bl.
Row 24: K2togbl, k17bl, k6sn. *(24 sts)*
Row 25: P6sn, p18bl.
Row 26: K18bl, k5sn, incsn. *(25 sts)*
Row 27: P7sn, p18bl.
Row 28: K2togbl, k15bl, k8sn. *(24 sts)*
Row 29: P8sn, p16bl.
Row 30: K2togbl, k14bl, k8sn. *(23 sts)*
Row 31: P8sn, p13bl, p2togbl. *(22 sts)*
Row 32: K2togbl, k11bl, k9sn. *(21 sts)*
Row 33: P9sn, p10bl, p2togbl. *(20 sts)*
Row 34: K2togbl, k9bl, k9sn. *(19 sts)*
Row 35: P9sn, p8bl, p2togbl. *(18 sts)*
Row 36: Bind off 7bl, k2bl ibos, k9sn (hold 11 sts on spare needle for Neck).

Head
An alert expression and a magnificent crop of whiskers add to this cat's streetwise personality.

Neck and Head

Row 1: With US 2 (2¾mm) needles and RS facing, k8sn, k3bl from spare needle of Right Side of Body, then k3bl, k8sn from spare needle of Left Side of Body. *(22 sts)*

Row 2: P4sn, p2togsn, p1sn, p8bl, p1sn, p2togsn, p4sn. *(20 sts)*

Row 3: K4sn, k12bl, k4sn.

Row 4: P3sn, p2togbl, p10bl, p2togbl, p3sn. *(18 sts)*

Row 5: K3sn, k12bl, wrap and turn.

Row 6: P12bl, w&t.

Row 7: K12bl, w&t.

Rep last 2 rows once more.

Row 10: P12bl, w&t.

Row 11: K12bl, k3sn. *(18 sts on right-hand needle)*

Row 12: P2sn, p14bl, p2sn.

Row 13: K2sn, k13bl, wrap and turn.

Row 14: P12bl, w&t.

Row 15: K12bl, w&t.

Rep last 2 rows once more.

Row 18: P12bl, w&t.

Row 19: K13bl, k2sn. *(18 sts on right-hand needle)*

Row 20: P2togsn, p1sn, p12bl, p1sn, p2togsn. *(16 sts)*

Row 21: K3sn, k4bl, k2togbl, k4bl, k3sn. *(15 sts)*

Row 22: P3sn, p2togbl, p2bl, p1sn, p2bl, p2togbl, p3sn. *(13 sts)*

Row 23: K3sn, k3bl, k1sn, k3bl, k3sn.

Row 24: P3sn, p2bl, p3sn, p2bl, p3sn.

Cont in sn.

Row 25: K3, k2tog, k3, k2tog, k3. *(11 sts)*

Row 26: Purl.

Row 27: K2, k2tog, k3, k2tog, k2. *(9 sts)*

Row 28: P2, p2tog, p1, p2tog, p2. *(7 sts)*

Bind off.

Tummy

With US 2 (2¾mm) needles and sn, cast on 3 sts.

Beg with a k row, work 8 rows st st.

Row 9: Inc, k1, inc. *(5 sts)*

Work 13 rows st st.

Row 23: Inc, k3, inc. *(7 sts)*

Work 3 rows st st.

Row 27: K2tog, k3, k2tog. *(5 sts)*

Work 3 rows st st.

Row 31: Inc, k3, inc. *(7 sts)*

Work 19 rows st st.

Row 51: K2tog, k3, k2tog. *(5 sts)*

Work 9 rows st st.

Row 61: K2tog, k1, k2tog. *(3 sts)*

Work 5 rows st st.

Row 67: K3tog and fasten off.

Ear

(make 2 the same)

With US 2 (2¾mm) needles and bl, cast on 6 sts.

Work 2 rows st st.

Row 3: K2tog, k2, k2tog. *(4 sts)*

Row 4: Purl.

Row 5: [K2tog] twice. *(2 sts)*

Row 6: P2tog and fasten off.

Tail

With 2¾mm (US 2) double-pointed needles and bl, cast on 9 sts.

Work in i-cord as follows:

Knit 12 rows.

Row 13: K2tog, k5, k2tog. *(7 sts)*

Knit 12 rows.

Row 26: K2tog, k3, k2tog. *(5 sts)*

Knit 1 row.

Change to sn.

Knit 4 rows.

Row 32: K2tog, k1, k2tog. *(3 sts)*

Row 33: K3tog and fasten off.

Collar

With US 2 (2¾mm) needles and fr, cast on 26 sts.

Knit 1 row.

Bind off.

To Finish

Sew in ends, leaving ends from bound off rows for sewing up. Using mattress or whip stitch, sew up legs starting at paw. Cut a pipecleaner to fit length of back leg, fold over the ends (so they don't poke out of the paws), and slip into leg. Lightly stuff and sew along top of back legs, then bend into shape as shown in photograph. Using mattress or whip stitch, sew along back of cat. At head, fold in half and sew bound off edges of nose together. Using mattress or whip stitch, sew cast on row of tummy to bottom end of cat and sew final row to nose. Ease and sew tummy to fit body, matching curves to front legs. Leave a 1in (2.5cm) gap on one side. Roll a pipecleaner in a small amount of stuffing and bend into a U shape. Fold over the ends (so they don't poke out of the paws) and slip into body down front legs. Stuff, and sew up gap with mattress stitch. Using whip stitch, attach back legs to body, sewing along top of leg and down back edge as shown in photograph. To hold the legs in place, at about ½in (1cm) down from top of leg, sew the inside of the leg to the body. Mold into shape. Attach the tail as in photograph. Sew ears to head, leaving about 3 sts between the two ears. For the eyes, use en yarn to make elongated French knots. Work each knot over 2 sts at a slight angle and wrap the yarn around the needle five times. With bl yarn, make a stitch over the center of the French knot. Using po yarn, embroider a small nose in satin stitch. For whiskers, cut 3in (8cm) strands of sewing thread and thread through cheeks, then trim. Slip optional bell onto collar, sew ends of collar together, then slide collar over head onto neck.

Tabby

One of the numerous erroneous beliefs regarding tabby cats is that the word 'tabby' means female. In fact, the name probably derives from the markings on watered silk originally made at Attabiy, in Baghdad. Tabbies are overachievers, holding numerous world records. These include heaviest cat, with Himmy weighing in at nearly 47lb (21.3kg); longest lived cat, with Ma reaching 34 years of age; most kittens, with Dusty giving birth to 420; and most toes, with Larry having 28.

Tabby Cat Prowling

Hugely adaptable, the shape of the Tabby makes this an ideal pattern for knitting any standard cat.

Measurements

Length: 8¾in (22cm)
Height to top of head: 4½in (11cm)

Materials

- Pair of US 2 (2¾mm) knitting needles
- 2 spare US 2 (2¾mm) knitting needles or small stitch holders or safety pins
- Pair of US 2 (2¾mm) double-pointed knitting needles
- 1oz (20g) of Rowan Felted Tweed in Cinnamon 175 (cn)
- ¼oz (10g) of Rowan Felted Tweed in Treacle 145 (te)
- Small amount of Rowan Pure Wool 4ply in Snow 412 (sn)
- Tiny amount of Rowan Cashsoft 4ply in Kiwi 443 (ki) for eyes
- Tiny amount of Rowan Pure Wool 4ply in Black 404 (bl) for pupils
- Tiny amount of Rowan Pure Wool 4ply in Powder 443 (po) for nose
- Small amount of Rowan Cashsoft 4ply in Cherish 453 (ch) for collar
- Bell for collar (optional)
- 3 pipecleaners
- Crochet hook
- Cream sewing thread for whiskers

Abbreviations

See page 141.
See page 141 for Wrap Method.
See page 141 for Stranding or Fair Isle Technique.

Right Back Leg

With US 2 (2¾mm) needles and sn, cast on 7 sts. Beg with a k row, work 2 rows st st.
Row 3: Inc, k2tog, k1, k2tog, inc. *(7 sts)*
Row 4: Purl.
Change to cn and te.
Row 5: Inccn, k2togcn, k1te, k2togte, incte.
Row 6: P4cn, p2te, p1cn. *(7 sts)*
Row 7: K1te, k6cn.
Row 8: P1cn, p4te, p2cn.
Row 9: Inccn, k1te, k4cn, incte. *(9 sts)*
Row 10: P2te, p7cn.
Row 11: K2togcn, k1cn, inccn, k1cn, inccn, k1cn, k2togcn. *(9 sts)*
Row 12: P2togte, p1te, incte, p1te, incte, p1te, p2togcn. *(9 sts)*
Row 13: K2togte, inccn into next 2 sts, k1cn, inccn into next 2 sts, k2togcn. *(11 sts)*
Row 14: P4cn, inccn, p1cn, inccn, p4cn. *(13 sts)*
Row 15: K5cn, inccn, k1cn, inccn, k4cn, wrap and turn.
Row 16: P6te, p7cn, w&t.
Row 17: K4cn, k1te, incte, k1te, incte, k3te, k1cn, w&t. *(14 sts)*
Row 18: P13cn, w&t.
Row 19: K5cn, inccn, k1cn, inccn, k2cn, k5te. *(19 sts in total)*
Row 20: P4cn, p5te, p10cn.
Row 21: K8cn, inccn, k1te, incte, k5cn, k3te. *(21 sts)*
Row 22: P4te, p17cn.
Row 23: K9cn, inccn, k1cn, inccn, k9cn. *(23 sts)*
Row 24: P6te, p17cn.
Row 25: Bind off 11 sts cn, k5cn ibos, k3te, k4cn (hold 12 sts on spare needle for Right Side of Body).

Left Back Leg

With US 2 (2¾mm) needles and sn, cast on 7 sts.
Beg with a k row, work 2 rows st st.
Row 3: Inc, k2tog, k1, k2tog, inc. *(7 sts)*
Row 4: Purl.
Change to cn and te.
Row 5: Incte, k2togte, k1te, k2togcn, inccn. *(7 sts)*
Row 6: P1cn, p2te, p4cn.
Row 7: K6cn, k1te.
Row 8: P2cn, p4te, p1cn.
Row 9: Incte, k4cn, k1te, inccn. *(9 sts)*
Row 10: P8cn, p1te.
Row 11: K2togcn, k1cn, inccn, k1cn, inccn, k1cn, k2togcn. *(9 sts)*
Row 12: P2togte, p1te, incte, p1te, incte, p1cn, p2togcn. *(9 sts)*
Row 13: K2togcn, inccn into next 2 sts, k1cn, inccn into next 2sts, k2togcn. *(11 sts)*
Row 14: P4cn, inccn, p1cn, inccn, p4cn. *(13 sts)*
Row 15: K3cn, inccn, k1cn, inccn, k1cn, inccn, k1, inccn, k3cn. *(17 sts)*
Row 16: P11cn, p6te.
Row 17: K3cn, k4te, incte, k1te, incte, k2te, k5cn. *(19 sts)*
Row 18: P19cn.
Row 19: K5te, k3cn, inccn, k1cn, inccn, k8cn. *(21 sts)*
Row 20: P11cn, p5te, p5cn.
Row 21: K3te, k6cn, incte, k1te, inccn, k9cn. *(23 sts)*
Row 22: P17cn, p6te.
Row 23: K6cn, k2te, k4cn, bind off 11 sts cn (hold 12 sts on spare needle for Left Side of Body).

Right Front Leg

With US 2 (2¾mm) needles and sn, cast on 7 sts.
Beg with a k row, work 2 rows st st.
Change to cn and te.

114

Row 3: Inccn, k2togcn, k1te, k2togte, incte. *(7 sts)*
Row 4: P3cn, p3te, p1cn.
Row 5: Incte, k2togcn, k1cn, k2togcn, inccn. *(7 sts)*
Row 6: P6cn, p1te.
Row 7: K7cn.
Row 8: P2cn, p5te.
Row 9: K4cn, k3te.
Row 10: P1te, p6cn.
Row 11: K7cn.
Row 12: P5te, p2cn.
Row 13: Incte, k1te, k4cn, inccn. *(9 sts)*
Row 14: P2te, p7cn.
Row 15: Inccn, k5cn, k2te, incte. *(11 sts)*
Row 16: P4cn, p3te, p4cn.
Row 18: Inccn, k4te, k5cn, inccn. *(13 sts)*
Row 18: P2cn, p4te, p4cn, p3te.*
Row 19: Bind off 6 sts cn, k7cn ibos (hold 7 sts on spare needle for Right Side of Body).

Left Front Leg
Work as for Right Front Leg to *.
Row 19: K7cn, bind off 6 sts cn (hold 7 sts on spare needle for Left Side of Body).

Right Side of Body
Row 1: With US 2 (2¾mm) needles and cn, cast on 1 st, k7 from spare needle of Right Front Leg, cast on 8 sts. *(16 sts)*
Join in te.
Row 2: P8cn, p1te, p7cn.
Row 3: Inccn, k1cn, k1te, k4cn, k1te, k2cn, k1te, k5cn, cast on 8 sts cn. *(25 sts)*
Row 4: P7cn, p1te, p4cn, p1te, p2cn, p1te, p4cn, p1te, p4cn.
Row 5: Incte, k1te, k3cn, k1te, k4cn, k1te, k2cn, k1te, k1cn, k1te, k2cn, k1te, k3cn, k1te, k2cn, then k7cn k2te, k3cn from spare needle of Right Back Leg, cast on 1 st cn. *(39 sts)*
Row 6: P4cn, p2te, p4cn, p1te, p3cn, p1te, p3cn, p1te, p2cn, p1te, p2cn, p1te, p2cn, p1te, p3cn, p1te, p3cn, p2te, p2cn.

Row 7: K3cn, k1te, k3cn, k2te, k2cn, k1te, k2cn, k2te, k1cn, k2te, k2cn, k1te, k3cn, k1te, k3cn, k1te, k4cn, k3te, k2cn.
Row 8: P2cn, p1te, p5cn, p1te, p3cn, p2te, p2cn, p2te, p2cn, p1te, p2cn, p2te, p2cn, p1te, p1cn, p2te, p3cn, p1te, p4cn.
Row 9: K2te, k2cn, k2te, k2cn, k4te, k2cn, k2te, k2cn, k1te, k2cn, k2te, k3cn, k1te, k4cn, k1te, k1cn, k1te, k3cn, k2te.
Row 10: P2te, p2cn, p1te, p2cn, p1te, p3cn, p2te, p2cn, p2te, p2cn, p1te, p2cn, p2te, p2cn, p3te, p3cn, p1te, p2cn, p3te.
Row 11: Place marker for Neck, k2togcn, k2te, k1cn, k1te, k3cn, k2te, k3cn, k2te, k2cn, k1te, k3cn, k2te, k2cn, k2te, k3cn, k1te, k2cn, k2te, k2cn, k1te. *(38 sts)*
Row 12: P3cn, p2te, p2cn, p1te, p3cn, p2te, p2cn, p2te, p2cn, p1te, p2cn, p2te, p2cn, p3te, p3cn, p2te, p2cn, p1te, p1cn, p1te, p2cn.
Row 13: K2togcn, k1te, k2cn, k1te, k2cn, k1te, k3cn, k2cn, k2te, k3cn, k2te, k2cn, k2te, k3cn, k1te, k3cn, k2te, k2cn. *(37 sts)*
Row 14: P1cn, p3te, p3cn, p1te, p3cn, p2te, p2cn, p3te, p2cn, p2te, p2cn, p2te, p2cn, p1te, p2cn, p1te, p1cn, p1te, p2cn.
Row 15: K2togcn, k1te, k1cn, k2te, k1cn, k1te, k1cn, k3te, k2cn, k2te, k3cn, k2te, k3cn, k2te, k2cn, k2te, k3cn, k4te. *(36 sts)*
Row 16: P5te, p3cn, p1te, p3cn, p2te, p2cn, p3te, p2cn, p3te, p2cn, p4te, p1cn, p2te, p1cn, p1te, p1cn.
Row 17: K2togte, k7te, k2cn, k3te, k2cn, k3cn, k2te, k3cn, k2te, k1te, k3cn, k4te, k2togte. *(34 sts)*
Row 18: P2togte, p4te, p2cn, p2te, p2cn, p3te, p2cn, p3te, p2cn, p12te. *(33 sts)*
Cont in te.
Row 19: Bind off 9 sts, k22, k2tog. *(23 sts)*
Bind off.

Left Side of Body

Row 1: With US 2 (2¾mm) needles and cn, cast on 1 st, p7 from spare needle of Left Front Leg, cast on 8 sts. *(16 sts)*
Join in te.

Row 2: K8cn, k1te, k7cn.

Row 3: Inccn, p1cn, p1te, p4cn, p1te, p2cn, p1te, p5cn, cast on 8 sts cn. *(25 sts)*

Row 4: K7cn, k1te, k4cn, k1te, k2cn, k1te, k4cn, k1te, k4cn.

Row 5: Incte, p1te, p3cn, p1te, p4cn, p1te, p2cn, p1te, p1cn, p1te, p2cn, p1te, p3cn, p1te, p2cn, then p7cn, p2te, p3cn from spare needle of Left Back Leg, cast on 1 st cn. *(39 sts)*

Row 6: K4cn, k2te, k4cn, k1te, k3cn, k1te, k3cn, k1te, k2cn, k1te, k2cn, k1te, k3cn, k1te, k3cn, k2te, k2cn.

Row 7: P3cn, p1te, p3cn, p2te, p2cn, p1te, p2cn, p2te, p1cn, p2te, p2cn, p1te, p3cn, p1te, p3cn, p1te, p4cn, p3te, p2cn.

Row 8: K2cn, k1te, k5cn, k1te, k3cn, k2te, k2cn, k2te, k2cn, k1te, k2cn, k2te, k2cn, k1te, k1cn, k2te, k3cn, k1te, k4cn.

Row 9: P2te, p2cn, p2te, p2cn, p4te, p2cn, p2te, p2cn, p1te, p2cn, p2te, p3cn, p1te, p4cn, p1te, p1cn, p1te, p3cn, p2te.

Row 10: K2te, k2cn, k1te, k2cn, k1te, k3cn, k2te, k2cn, k2te, k3cn, k1te, k2cn, k2te, k2cn, k3te, k3cn, k1te, k2cn, k3te.

Row 11: Place marker for Neck, p2togcn, p2te, p1cn, p1te, p3cn, p2te, p3cn, p2te, p2cn, p1te, p3cn, p2te, p2cn, p2te, p3cn, p1te, p2cn, p2te, p2cn, p1te. *(38 sts)*

Row 12: K3cn, k2te, k2cn, k1te, k3cn, k2te, k2cn, k2te, k3cn, k1te, k2cn, k3te, k2cn, k2te, k2cn, k2te, k1cn, k1te, k2cn.

Row 13: P2togcn, p1te, p2cn, p1te, p2cn, p1te, p3cn, p2te, p2cn, p2te, p3cn, p2te, p2cn, p2te, p3cn, p1te, p3cn, p2te, p2cn. *(37 sts)*

Row 14: K1cn, k3te, k3cn, k1te, k3cn, k2te, k2cn, k3te, k2cn, k2te, k3cn, k2te, k2cn, k1te, k2cn, k1te, k1cn, k1te, k2cn.

Row 15: P2togcn, p1te, p1cn, p2te, p1cn, p1te, p1cn, p3te, p2cn, p2te, p3cn, p2te, p3cn, p2te, p2cn, p2te, p3cn, p4te. *(36 sts)*

Row 16: K5te, k3cn, k1te, k3cn, k2te, k3te, k2cn, k3te, k2cn, k4te, k1cn, k2te, k1cn, k1te, k1cn.

Row 17: P2togte, p7te, p2cn, p3te, p2cn, p3te, p2cn, p3te, p2cn, p1te, p3cn, p4te, p2togte. *(34 sts)*

Row 18: K2togte, k4te, k2cn, k2te, k2cn, k3te, k2cn, k3te, k2cn, k12te. *(33 sts)*
Cont in te.

Row 19: Bind off 9 sts, p22, p2tog. *(23 sts)*
Bind off.

Neck and Head

Row 1: With US 2 (2¾mm) needles and cn and RS facing, pick up 8 sts between marker and bound off edge of Right Side of Body, then pick up 8 sts between bound off edge of Left Side of Body and marker. *(16 sts)*
Join in te.

Row 2: P4cn, p1te, p1cn, p1te, p2cn, p1te, p1cn, p1te, p4cn.

Row 3: K3cn, k1te, inccn, k1cn, k1te, k2cn, k1te, k1cn, inccn, k1te, k3cn. *(18 sts)*

Row 4: P2cn, p1te, p4cn, p1te, p2cn, p1te, p4cn, p1te, p2cn.

Row 5: K1cn, k1te, k4cn, k1te, k4cn, k1te, k3cn, wrap and turn.

Row 6: P3cn, p1te, p4cn, p1te, p3cn, w&t.

Row 7: K3cn, k1te, k4cn, k1te, k3cn, w&t.
Rep last 2 rows once more.

Row 10: P5cn, p2te, p5cn, w&t.

Row 11: K5cn, k2te, k6cn, k1te, k1cn.
(18 sts on right-hand needle)

Row 12: P7cn, p1te, p2cn, p1te, p7cn.

Row 13: K1cn, k2te, k4cn, k1te, k2cn, k1te, k4cn, wrap and turn.

Row 14: P2cn, p1te, p1cn, p1te, p2cn, p1te, p1cn, p1te, p2cn, w&t.

Row 15: K2cn, k1te, k1cn, k1te, k2cn, k1te, k1cn, k1te, k2cn, w&t.
Rep last 2 rows once more.

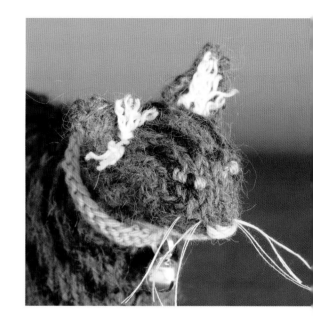

Markings

The 'M' shape and spectacle markings on the head are typical for a tabby cat.

Row 18: P1cn, p1te, p3cn, p2te, p3cn, p1te, p1cn, w&t.
Row 19: K2te, k8cn, k4te, k1cn. *(18 sts on right-hand needle)*
Row 20: P2togcn, p2cn, p2togcn, p1te, p1cn, p2togcn, p1cn, p1te, p2togcn, p2cn, p2togcn. *(13 sts)*
Cont in cn.
Row 21: K3, k2tog, k3, k2tog, k3. *(11 sts)*
Row 22: P2, p2tog, p3, p2tog, p2. *(9 sts)*
Row 23: K2, k2tog, k1, k2tog, k2. *(7 sts)*
Bind off.

Tummy

With US 2 (2¾mm) needles and cn, cast on 3 sts.
Beg with a k row, work 16 rows st st.
Row 17: Inc, k1, inc. *(5 sts)*
Work 23 rows st st.
Row 41: K2tog, k1, k2tog. *(3 sts)*
Work 11 rows st st.
Join in te.
Work 2 rows st st in te.
Work 3 rows st st in cn.
Work 2 rows st st in te.
Work 2 rows st st in cn.
Join in sn.
Row 62: K1cn, k1sn, k1cn.
Row 63: P1cn, p1sn, p1cn.
Cont in sn.
Work 16 rows st st.
Row 80: K3tog and fasten off.

Tail

With US 2 (2¾mm) double-pointed needles and te, cast on 6 sts.
Work in i-cord as follows:
Knit 4 rows.
Join in cn.
Row 5: K1cn, k4te, k1cn.
Row 6: K2cn, k2te, k2cn.
Row 7: K6cn.
Row 8: K2cn, k2te, k2cn.
Row 9: K1cn, k4te, k1cn.

Knit 2 rows in te.
Rep rows 5–11 twice more.
Cont in cn.
Knit 2 rows.
Row 28: K2tog, k4, k2tog. *(4 sts)*
Knit 2 rows.
Row 31: [K2tog] twice.
Row 32: K2tog and fasten off.

Ear

(make 2 the same)
With US 2 (2¾mm) needles and cn, cast on 6 sts.
Beg with a k row, work 2 rows st st.
Row 3: K2tog, k2, k2tog. *(4 sts)*
Work 2 rows st st.
Row 6: [P2tog] twice. *(2 sts)*
Row 7: K2tog and fasten off.

Collar

With US 2 (2¾mm) needles and ch, cast on 28 sts.
Knit 1 row.
Bind off.

To Finish

Sew in ends, leaving ends from bound off rows for sewing up. Using mattress or whip stitch, sew up legs starting at paw. Using mattress or whip stitch, sew along back of cat and down bottom. At head, fold in half and sew bound off edges of nose together. Using mattress or whip stitch, sew cast on row of tummy to bottom end of cat and sew final row to nose. Ease and sew tummy to fit body. Leave a 1in (2.5cm) gap between front and back legs on one side. Roll two pipecleaners in a small amount of stuffing and bend each one into a U shape. Fold over the ends (so they don't poke out of the paws) and slip into body, one pipecleaner down front legs and one down back legs. Stuff, and sew up gap with mattress stitch. Mold into shape. Cut a pipecleaner to length of tail, plus a small amount in order to fold over the ends. Insert pipecleaner into tail and attach the tail as in photograph. Sew ears to head, leaving about 3 sts between the two ears. Using a crochet hook and 2 strands of unplied sn yarn, on the inside of each ear make two tufts. For the eyes, use ki yarn to make elongated French knots. Work each knot over 2 sts at a slight angle and wrap the yarn around the needle five times. With bl yarn, make a stitch over the center of the French knot. Using po yarn, embroider a small nose in satin stitch. For whiskers, cut 3in (8cm) strands of sewing thread and thread through cheeks, then trim. Slip optional bell onto collar, sew ends of collar together, then slide collar over head onto neck.

Tabby Curled Up

When you knit the wrap & turn sections on the body of this cat, you move in one stitch at the beginning of each row, as described in the pattern.

Measurements
Length: 5¼in (13cm)

Materials
- Pair of US 2 (2¾mm) knitting needles
- Pair of US 2 (2¾mm) double-pointed knitting needles
- ½oz (15g) of Rowan Felted Tweed in Carbon 159 (ca)
- ¼oz (10g) of Rowan Felted Tweed in Treacle 145 (te)
- ⅛oz (5g) of Rowan Kidsilk Haze in Ghost 642 (gh) used DOUBLE throughout
- Tiny amount of Rowan Cashsoft 4ply in Almond 458 (al) for eyes
- Tiny amount of Rowan Pure Wool 4ply in Black 404 (bl) for pupils and nose
- Rice or lentils for stuffing
- Transparent nylon thread for whiskers
- 1 pipecleaner

Abbreviations
See page 141.
See page 141 for Wrap Method.
See page 141 for Stranding or Fair Isle Technique.

Back Leg
With US 2 (2¾mm) needles and ca, cast on 7 sts.
Beg with a k row, work 4 rows st st.
Join in te.
Row 5: K4te, k3ca.
Row 6: P3te, p4ca.
Work 3 rows st st in ca.
Row 10: P3te, p4ca.
Row 11: K4te, k3ca.
Cont in ca.
Row 12: Purl.
Row 13: Inc, k1, inc, k1, inc, k1, inc. *(11 sts)*
Row 14: P6te, p5ca.
Row 15: K3ca, k1te, incte, k1te, incte, k4te. *(13 sts)*
Row 16: P12te, p1ca.
Row 17: K5te, incte, k1te, incte, k5te. *(15 sts)*
Row 18: P4te, p11ca.
Row 19: K6ca, incca, k1ca, incca, k6ca. *(17 sts)*
Row 20: P9ca, p8te.
Row 21: K7te, incte, k1te, incte, k1te, k6ca. *(19 sts)*
Row 22: P14ca, p5te.
Row 23: K16te, k3ca.
Row 24: P14ca, p5te.
Row 25: K10ca, k9te.
Row 26: P3te, p16ca.
Row 27: K7ca, k2togca, k1ca, k2togca, k7ca. *(17 sts)*
Row 28: P6ca, p2togca, p1ca, p2togca, p6ca. *(15 sts)*
Row 29: K5ca, k2togca, k1ca, k2togca, k5ca. *(13 sts)*
Bind off 5te and 8ca.

Body and Head
(knitted in one piece)
With US 2 (2¾mm) needles and ca, cast on 20 sts.
Row 1: Knit.
Join in te.
Row 2: P9ca, p2te, p9ca.
Row 3: K8ca, incca, k2te, incca, k8ca. *(22 sts)*
Row 4: P4ca, p4te, p2ca, p2te, p2ca, p4te, p4ca.
Row 5: K2ca, k6te, k1ca, incca, k2te, incca, k1ca, k6te, k2ca. *(24 sts)*
Row 6: P6ca, p4te, p1ca, p2te, p1ca, p4te, p6ca.
Row 7: K10ca, incca, k2te, incca, k10ca. *(26 sts)*
Row 8: P6ca, p5te, p1ca, p2te, p1ca, p5te, p6ca.
Row 9: K2ca, k1te, k2ca, k6te, k1ca, k2te, k1ca, k6te, k2ca, k1te, wrap and turn.
Row 10: P1te, p4ca, p3te, p2ca, p2te, p2ca, p3te, p4ca, p1te, w&t. *(22 sts)*
Row 11: K9ca, incca, k2te, incca, k8ca, w&t. *(23 sts)*
Row 12: P3ca, p6te, p1ca, p2te, p1ca, p6te, p3ca, w&t. *(22 sts)*
Row 13: K21te, w&t. *(21 sts)*
Row 14: P20te, w&t. *(20 sts)*
Row 15: K3te, k3ca, k2te, incte, k2te, incte, k2te, k3ca, k2te, w&t. *(21 sts)*
Row 16: P6ca, p8te, p6ca, w&t. *(20 sts)*
Row 17: K7ca, k6te, k6ca, w&t. *(19 sts)*
Row 18: P2ca, p2te, p3ca, p4te, p3ca, p2te, p2ca, w&t. *(18 sts)*
Row 19: K5te, k3ca, k2te, k3ca, k5te, k6ca. *(30 sts on right-hand needle)*
Row 20: P4ca, p4te, p3ca, p1te, p2ca, p2te, p2ca, p1te, p3ca, p4te, p4ca.
Row 21: K3ca, k4te, k4ca, k1te, k1ca, incca, k2te, incca, k1ca, k1te, k4ca, k4te, k3ca. *(32 sts)*
Row 22: P3ca, p3te, p6ca, p1te, p2ca, p2te, p2ca, p1te, p6ca, p3te, p3ca.
Row 23: Incca, k1ca, k2te, k11ca, k2te, k11ca, k2te, k1ca, incca. *(34 sts)*
Join in gh.
Row 24: P1gh, p1ca, p2te, p4ca, p3te, p5ca, p2te, p5ca, p3te, p4ca, p2te, p1ca, p1gh.
Row 25: K1gh, k5ca, k6te, k4ca, k2te, k4ca, k6te, k4ca, wrap and turn. *(32 sts)*

Row 26: P3ca, p8te, k3ca, p2te, p3ca, p8te, p3ca, w&t. *(30 sts)*

Row 27: K2ca, k3te, k4ca, k3te, k1ca, incca, k2te, incca, k1ca, k3te, k4ca, k3te, k1ca, w&t. *(31 sts)*

Row 28: P1ca, p2te, p5ca, p3te, p3ca, p2te, p3ca, p4te, p5ca, p2te, w&t. *(30 sts)*

Row 29: K1te, k2ca, k1te, k2ca, k4te, k4ca, k2te, k4ca, k4te, k2ca, k1te, k2ca, w&t. *(29 sts)*

Row 30: P4ca, p5te, p4ca, p2te, p4ca, p5te, p4ca, w&t. *(28 sts)*

Row 31: K13ca, k2te, k12ca, w&t. *(27 sts)*

Row 32: P1te, p10ca, p4te, p10ca, p1te, w&t. *(26 sts)*

Row 33: K4te, k5ca, k8te, k4ca, k6te, k2ca, k2gh. *(36 sts)*

Row 34: P2gh, p4ca, p10te, p1ca, p2te, p1ca, p10te, p4ca, p2gh.

Row 35: K2gh, k5ca, k8te, k2ca, k2te, k2ca, k8te, k5ca, k2gh.

Row 36: P3gh, p7ca, p4te, p3ca, p2te, p3ca, p4te, p7ca, p3gh.

Row 37: K3gh, k3ca, k1te, k6ca, k2te, k2ca, k2te, k2ca, k2te, k6ca, k1te, k3ca, k1gh, wrap and turn. *(34 sts)*

Row 38: P1gh, p4ca, p1te, p9ca, p2te, p9ca, p1te, p4ca, p1gh, w&t. *(32 sts)*

Row 39: K2gh, k4ca, k2te, k7ca, k2te, k7ca, k2te, k4ca, k1gh, w&t. *(31 sts)*

Row 40: P1gh, p5ca, p6te, p2ca, p2te, p2ca, p6te, p5ca, p1gh, w&t. *(30 sts)*

Row 41: K1gh, k7ca, k4te, k2togca, k2te, k2togca, k4te, k7ca, w&t. *(27 sts)*

Row 42: P2ca, p2te, p5ca, p8te, p5ca, p2te, p2ca, w&t. *(26 sts)*

Row 43: K2ca, k1te, k5ca, k2te, k2togte, k2te, k2togte, k1te, k5ca, k2te, k1ca, w&t. *(23 sts)*

Row 44: P2ca, p1te, p7ca, p2te, p7ca, p2te, p1ca. *(22 sts)*

Row 45: K2ca, k2te, k4ca, k2togca, k2te, k2togca, k2ca, k2te, k5ca, k4gh. *(30 sts)*

Row 46: P4gh, p6ca, p2te, p2ca, p2te, p2ca, p2te, p6ca, p4gh.

Body
Use the stranding or Fair Isle method for knitting the stripes of this tabby cat, which has the traditional mackerel patterning.

Back
To make him lie more realistically,
our curled up tabby has only one leg.

Row 47: K2toggh, k3gh, k5ca, k2te, k2togte, k2te, k2togte, k2te, k5ca, k3gh, k2toggh. *(26 sts)*

Row 48: P4gh, p1ca, p1te, p4ca, p6te, p4ca, p1te, p1ca, p4gh.

Row 49: K2toggh, k3gh, k1ca, k1te, k2ca, k1te, k2togte, k2te, k2togte, k1te, k2ca, k1te, k1ca, k3gh, k2toggh. *(22 sts)*

Row 50: P2toggh, p2gh, p2ca, p10te, p2ca, p2gh, p2toggh. *(20 sts)*

Row 51: K2toggh, k1gh, k3ca, k1te, k2togte, k2te, k2togte, k1te, k3ca, k1gh, k2toggh. *(16 sts)*

Row 52: P2gh, p5ca, p2te, p5ca, p2gh.

Row 53: K2gh, k1ca, k2te, k1ca, incca, k2te, incca, k1ca, k2te, k1ca, k2gh. *(18 sts)*

Row 54: P2gh, p2ca, p3te, incte, p2te, incte, p3te, p2ca, p2gh. *(20 sts)*

Row 55: K2gh, k4ca, k8te, k2ca, wrap and turn.

Row 56: P4ca, p4te, p4ca, w&t.

Row 57: K5ca, k2te, k5ca, w&t.

Row 58: P2te, p3ca, p2te, p3ca, p2te, w&t.

Row 59: K2ca, k8te, k2ca, w&t.

Row 60: P5ca, p2te, p5ca, w&t.

Row 61: K1ca, k1te, k1ca, k1te, k4ca, k1te, k1ca, k1te, k3ca, k2gh. *(20 sts on right-hand needle)*

Row 62: P2gh, p2ca, p1te, p1ca, p1te, p1ca, p1te, p2ca, p1ca, p1te, p1ca, p1te, p2ca, p2gh.

Row 63: K2gh, k2ca, k1te, k1ca, k1te, k2ca, k2te, k2ca, k1te, k2ca, wrap and turn.

Row 64: P1ca, p1te, p3ca, p2te, p3ca, p1te, p1ca, w&t.

Row 65: K1ca, k1te, k3ca, k2te, k3ca, k1te, k1ca, w&t.

Row 66: P12ca, w&t.

Row 67: K14ca, k2gh. *(20 sts in total)*

Row 68: P2toggh, p2ca, p2togca, p1ca, p2togca, p2ca, p2togca, p1ca, p2togca, p2ca, p2toggh. *(14 sts)*

Row 69: K1gh, k1ca, k2togca, k1ca, [k2togca] twice, k1ca, k2togca, k1ca, k1gh. *(10 sts)*

Row 70: P2ca, p2togca, p2ca, p2togca, p2ca. *(8 sts)*

Row 71: [K2togca] 4 times. *(4 sts)*
Bind off.

Ear

(make 2 the same)
With US 2 (2¾mm) needles and ca, cast on 6 sts.
Work 2 rows st st.

Row 3: K2tog, k2, k2tog. *(4 sts)*

Row 4: Purl.

Row 5: [K2tog] twice. *(2 sts)*

Row 6: P2tog and fasten off.

Tail

With US 2 (2¾mm) double-pointed needles and ca, cast on 6 sts.
Work in i-cord as follows:
Knit 4 rows.
Join in te.

Row 5: K1te, k4ca, k1te.

Row 6: K2te, k2ca, k2te.

Row 7: K6te.

Row 8: K2te, k2ca, k2te.

Row 9: K1te, k4ca, k1te.
Knit 2 rows in ca.
Rep rows 5–11 twice more.
Cont in ca.

Row 26: K2tog, k2, k2tog. *(4 sts)*
Knit 2 rows.

Row 29: [K2tog] twice. *(2 sts)*

Row 30: K2tog and fasten off.

To Finish

Sew in ends, leaving ends from bound off rows for sewing up. Using mattress or whip stitch, sew up leg starting at paw. Using mattress or whip stitch, sew along tummy and head, leaving a 1in (2.5cm) gap. Cut a pipecleaner to just longer than cat, fold over the ends, and slip into body and head. The pipecleaner is useful for adding to the curved back and head position. Stuff with rice or lentils to give the cat more weight, and sew up gap with mattress stitch. Mold into shape. Attach leg and tail as in photograph. With a little stitch, attach the paw and the tip of tail to body. Sew ears to head, leaving about 3 sts between the two ears. For the eyes, use al yarn to make elongated French knots. Work each knot over 2 sts at a slight angle and wrap the yarn around the needle five times. With bl yarn, make a stitch over the center of the French knot. Using bl yarn, embroider a small nose in satin stitch. For whiskers, cut 3in (8cm) strands of transparent nylon and thread through cheeks, then trim.

Black Cat

Cardinal Richelieu, the French clergyman of *Three Musketeers* fame, had a jet black cat called Lucifer. The British King Charles I, who was tried for treason and executed in 1649, had a black cat called Luck who died the day before he was arrested. The witch's companion, the black cat is supposed to bring luck (unless you're Charles I). Some people believe black cats to be witches incarnate, and the cats were often used as familiars. Isaac Newton's black cat Spitface interrupted him so frequently, wanting to be let out, that Newton was forced to invent the cat flap.

Black Cat Prowling

A simple, sleek, easy-to-knit prowling cat.

Measurements
Length: 7½in (19cm)
Height to top of head: 4in (10cm)

Materials
- Pair of US 2 (2¾mm) knitting needles
- 4 spare US 2 (2¾mm) knitting needles or small stitch holders or safety pins
- Pair of US 2 (2¾mm) double-pointed knitting needles
- 1oz (20g) of Rowan Cashsoft 4ply in Black 422 (bl)
- Small amount of Cashsoft 4ply in Cherish 453 (ch) for collar
- Tiny amount of Rowan Pure Wool 4ply in Gerbera 454 (ge) for eyes
- 3 pipecleaners
- Black sewing thread for whiskers
- Bell for collar (optional)

Abbreviations
See page 141.
See page 141 for Wrap Method.
See page 141 for Intarsia Technique.

Right Back Leg
With US 2 (2¾mm) needles and bl, cast on 7 sts.
Beg with a k row, work 2 rows st st.
Row 3: Inc, k2tog, k1, k2tog, inc. *(7 sts)*
Row 4: Purl.
Rep last 2 rows once more.
Work 2 rows st st.
Row 9: K2, inc, k1, inc, k2. *(9 sts)*

Row 10: Purl.
Row 11: K2tog, inc into next 2 sts, k1, inc into next 2 sts, k2tog. *(11 sts)*
Row 12: P2tog, p2, inc, p1, inc, p2, p2tog. *(11 sts)*
Row 13: K2tog, inc, k1, inc, k1, inc, k1, inc, k2tog. *(13 sts)*
Row 14: Purl.*
Row 15: K5, inc, k1, inc, k4, wrap and turn.
Row 16: P13, w&t.
Row 17: K5, inc, k1, inc, k4, w&t. *(14 sts)*
Row 18: P13, w&t.
Row 19: K5, inc, k1, inc, k7. *(19 sts in total)*
Row 20: Purl.
Row 21: K8, inc, k1, inc, k8. *(21 sts)*
Row 22: Purl.
Row 23: K9, inc, k1, inc, k9. *(23 sts)*
Work 3 rows st st.
Row 27: Bind off 11 sts, k to end (hold 12 sts on spare needle for Right Side of Body).

Left Back Leg
Work as for Right Back Leg to *.
Row 15: K3, inc, k1, inc, k1, inc, k1, inc, k3. *(17 sts)*
Row 16: Purl.
Row 17: K7, inc, k1, inc, k7. *(19 sts)*
Row 18: Purl.
Row 19: K8, inc, k1, inc, k8. *(21 sts)*
Row 20: Purl.
Row 21: K9, inc, k1, inc, k9. *(23 sts)*
Work 3 rows st st.
Row 25: K12, bind off 11 sts (hold 12 sts on spare needle for Left Side of Body).

Right Front Leg
With US 2 (2¾mm) needles and bl, cast on 7 sts.
Beg with a k row, work 2 rows st st.
Row 3: Inc, k2tog, k1, k2tog, inc. *(7 sts)*
Row 4: Purl.
Rep last 2 rows once more.
Work 6 rows st st.
Row 13: Inc, k5, inc. *(9 sts)*

Row 14: Purl.
Row 15: K3, inc, k1, inc, k3. *(11 sts)*
Row 16: Purl.
Row 17: K4, inc, k1, inc, k4. *(13 sts)*
Row 18: Purl.
Row 19: K5, inc, k1, inc, k5. *(15 sts)*
Row 20: Purl.
Row 21: K6, inc, k1, inc, k6. *(17 sts)*
Row 22: Purl.**
Row 23: Bind off 8 sts, k9 (hold 9 sts on spare needle for Right Side of Body).

Left Front Leg
Work as for Right Front Leg to **.
Row 23: K9, bind off 8 sts (hold 9 sts on spare needle for Left Side of Body).

Right Side of Body
Row 1: With US 2 (2¾mm) needles and bl, cast on 1 st, with RS facing k9 from spare needle of Right Front Leg, cast on 7 sts. *(17 sts)*
Row 2: Purl.
Row 3: Inc, k16, cast on 8 sts. *(26 sts)*
Row 4: Purl.
Row 5: K26, with RS facing k12 from spare needle of Right Back Leg, cast on 1 st. *(39 sts)*
Row 6: Purl.
Row 7: Inc, k38. *(40 sts)*
Work 4 rows st st.
Row 12: P38, p2tog. *(39 sts; place contrast marker at neck end)*
Row 13: Knit.
Row 14: P37, p2tog. *(38 sts)*
Row 15: Knit.
Row 16: P36, p2tog. *(37 sts)*
Row 17: K35, k2tog. *(36 sts)*
Row 18: P2tog, p32, p2tog. *(34 sts)*
Row 19: Bind off 10 sts, k22 ibos, k2tog. *(23 sts)*
Bind off.

Tail

Bend the tail into a gentle 'S' shape
to balance the cat.

Left Side of Body

Row 1: With US 2 (2¾mm) needles and bl, cast on 1 st, with WS facing p9 from spare needle of Right Front Leg, cast on 7 sts. *(17 sts)*

Row 2: Knit.

Row 3: Inc, p16, cast on 8 sts. *(26 sts)*

Row 4: Knit.

Row 5: P26, with WS facing p12 from spare needle of Right Back Leg, cast on 1 st. *(39 sts)*

Row 6: Knit.

Row 7: Inc, p38. *(40 sts)*

Work 4 rows st st.

Row 12: K38, k2tog. *(39 sts; place contrast marker at neck end)*

Row 13: Purl.

Row 14: K37, k2tog. *(38 sts)*

Row 15: Purl.

Row 16: K36, k2tog. *(37 sts)*

Row 17: P35, p2tog. *(36 sts)*

Row 18: K2tog, k32, k2tog. *(34 sts)*

Row 19: Bind off 10 sts, p22 ibos, p2tog. *(23 sts)*

Bind off.

Neck and Head

Row 1: With US 2 (2¾mm) needles and bl and RS facing, cast on 1 st, pick up 7 sts from row ends at neck from marker of Right Side of Body, then 7 sts from row ends at neck to marker of Left Side of Body, cast on 1 st. *(16 sts)*

Row 2: Purl.

Row 3: K4, inc, k6, inc, k4. *(18 sts)*

Row 4: Purl.

Row 5: K15, wrap and turn (leave rem 3 sts on left-hand needle unworked).

Row 6: Working top of head on center 12 sts only, p12, w&t.

Row 7: K12, w&t.

Rep last 2 rows once more.

Row 10: P12, w&t.

Row 11: K15. *(18 sts on right-hand needle)*

Head

We have given our cat yellow eyes,
but green, or even blue, eyes would
look wonderful with the jet black fur.

Row 12: Purl.
Row 13: K15, wrap and turn.
Row 14: P12, w&t.
Row 15: K12, w&t.
Rep last 2 rows once more.
Row 18: P12, w&t.
Row 19: K15. *(18 sts on right-hand needle)*
Row 20: [P2tog, p2] 4 times, p2tog. *(13 sts)*
Row 21: K3, k2tog, k3, k2tog, k3. *(11 sts)*
Row 22: P2, p2tog, p3, p2tog, p2. *(9 sts)*
Row 23: Knit.
Row 24: P2, p2tog, p1, p2tog, p2. *(7 sts)*
Bind off.

Tummy

With US 2 (2¾mm) needles and bl, cast on
3 sts.
Beg with a k row, work 15 rows st st.
Row 16: Inc, p1, inc. *(5 sts)*
Work 50 rows st st.
Row 67: K2tog, k1, k2tog. *(3 sts)*
Work 3 rows st st.
Row 71: K3tog and fasten off.

Ear

(make 2 the same)
With US 2 (2¾mm) needles and bl, cast on
6 sts.
Beg with a k row, work 2 rows st st.
Row 3: K2tog, k2, k2tog. *(4 sts)*
Row 4: Purl.
Row 5: [K2tog] twice. *(2 sts)*
Row 6: P2tog and fasten off.

Tail

With US 2 (2¾mm) double-pointed needles
and bl, cast on 6 sts.
Work in i-cord as follows:
Knit 20 rows.
Row 21: K2tog, k2, k2tog. *(4 sts)*
Knit 6 rows.
Row 28: [K2tog] twice. *(2 sts)*
Row 29: K2tog and fasten off.

Collar

With US 2 (2¾mm) needles and ch, cast on
26 sts.
Knit 1 row.
Bind off.

To Finish

Sew in ends, leaving ends from bound off
rows for sewing up. Using mattress or whip
stitch, sew up legs starting at paw. Using
mattress or whip stitch, sew along back of
cat and down bottom. At head, fold in half
and sew bound off edges of nose together.
Using mattress or whip stitch, sew cast on
row of tummy to bottom end of cat and sew
final row to nose. Ease and sew tummy to
fit body. Leave a 1in (2.5cm) gap between
front and back legs on one side. Roll the
pipecleaners in a small amount of stuffing
and bend each one into a U shape. Fold over
the ends (so they don't poke out of the paws)
and slip into body, one pipecleaner down
front legs and one down back legs. Stuff,
and sew up gap with mattress stitch. Mold
into shape. Cut a pipecleaner to length of
tail, plus a small amount in order to fold
over the ends. Slip pipecleaner into tail and
sew tail together on the underside. Attach to
bottom as in photograph. Sew ears to head,
leaving about 3 sts between the two ears.
For the eyes, use ge yarn to make elongated
French knots. Work each knot over 2 sts
at a slight angle and wrap the yarn around
the needle five times. With bl yarn, make a
stitch over the center of the French knot.
For whiskers, cut 3in (8cm) strands of
sewing thread and thread through cheeks,
then trim. Slip optional bell onto collar, sew
ends of collar together, then slide collar over
head onto neck.

Tortoiseshell

The serial killer cat, a tortoiseshell called Towser is the champion mouser of all time. Owned by the Glenturret Distillery in Tayside, Scotland, she is estimated to have killed a total of 28,899 rodents in her lifetime. Tortoiseshell cats are more often—but not exclusively—female, and the males are possessed of unusual and interesting powers. Apparently, rubbing the tail of a male tortoiseshell cat will cure your warts, but only in May.

Tortoiseshell Cat Lying Down

Simple and rewarding to knit, ours is a brindle-colored tortoiseshell cat.

Measurements

Length: 6in (15cm)
Height to top of head: 3½in (9cm)

Materials

- Pair of US 2 (2¾mm) knitting needles
- 4 spare US 2 (2¾mm) knitting needles or small stitch holders or safety pins
- Pair of US 2 (2¾mm) double-pointed knitting needles
- ⅛oz (5g) of Rowan Pure Wool 4ply in Snow 412 (sn)
- ½oz (15g) of Rowan Felted Tweed in Treacle 145 (te)
- ¼oz (10g) of Rowan Kidsilk Haze in Ember 644 (em)
- NOTE: Use 1 strand of te and 1 strand of em TOGETHER throughout
- Tiny amount of Rowan Cashsoft 4ply in Almond 458 (al) for eyes
- Tiny amount of Rowan Pure Wool 4ply in Black 404 (bl) for pupils
- 3 pipecleaners
- Rice or lentils for stuffing
- Cream sewing thread for whiskers

Abbreviations

See page 141.
See page 141 for Wrap Method.
See page 141 for Intarsia Technique.

Right Back Leg

With US 2 (2¾mm) needles and sn, cast on 7 sts.
Beg with a k row, work 6 rows st st.
Change to te and em.
Work 2 rows st st.
Row 9: K2, inc, k1, inc, k2. *(9 sts)*
Row 10: Purl.
Row 11: [Inc, k1] 4 times, inc. *(14 sts)*
Row 12: Purl.
Row 13: [Inc, k1] 7 times.* *(21 sts)*
Row 14: P11, bind off 10 sts (hold 11 sts on spare needle for Right Side of Body).

Left Back Leg

Work as for Right Back Leg to *.
Row 14: Bind off 10 sts, p to end (hold 11 sts on spare needle for Left Side of Body).

Right Front Leg

With US 2 (2¾mm) needles and sn, cast on 7 sts.
Beg with a k row, work 4 rows st st.
Change to te and em.
Work 8 rows st st.
Row 13: K2, inc, k1, inc, k2. *(9 sts)*
Row 14: Purl.
Row 15: K4, wrap and turn.
Row 16: P4.
Row 17: K3, w&t.
Row 18: P3.
Row 19: K2, w&t.
Row 20: P2.
Row 21: K1, w&t.
Row 22: P1.
Row 23: K to end. *(9 sts)*
Row 24: P4, w&t (leave rem 5 sts on left-hand needle unworked).
Cont working on 4 sts only.
Row 25: K4.
Row 26: P4, w&t.
Row 27: K3.
Row 28: P3, w&t.
Row 29: K2.
Row 30: P2, w&t.
Row 31: K1.
Row 32: P to end. *(9 sts)*
Row 33: K3, inc, k1, inc, k3. *(11 sts)*
Row 34: Purl.**
Row 35: Bind off 5 sts, k to end (hold 6 sts on spare needle for Right Side of Body).

Left Front Leg

Work as for Right Front Leg to **.
Row 35: K6, bind off 5 sts (hold 6 sts on spare needle for Left Side of Body).

Right Side of Body

Row 1: With US 2 (2¾mm) needles and te and em, cast on 2 sts, k6 from spare needle of Right Front Leg, cast on 8 sts, k11 from spare needle of Right Back Leg, cast on 3 sts. *(30 sts)*
Row 2: P14, k1, p15.
Row 3: Inc, k14, p1, k14. *(31 sts)*
Row 4: P14, k1, p16.
Row 5: Inc, k16, p1, k13. *(32 sts)*
Row 6: P13, k1, p18.
Row 7: Inc, k17, p1, k11, k2tog. *(32 sts)*
Row 8: P11, k1, p20.
Row 9: K20, p1, k9, k2tog. *(31 sts)*
Row 10: P9, k1, p21.
Row 11: K22, p1, k6, k2tog. *(30 sts)*
Row 12: P1, k6, p23.
Row 13: K28, k2tog. *(29 sts)*
Row 14: Purl.
Row 15: K9 (hold these 9 sts on spare needle for Neck), k2tog, k16, k2tog. *(18 sts)*
Row 16: Bind off 2 sts, p14 ibos, p2tog. *(15 sts)*
Row 17: Bind off 2 sts, k11 ibos, k2tog. *(12 sts)*
Row 18: Bind off 2 sts, p8 ibos, p2tog. *(9 sts)*
Row 19: Bind off 2 sts, k5 ibos, k2tog. *(6 sts)*
Bind off.

Left Side of Body

Row 1: With US 2 (2¾mm) needles and te and em, cast on 2 sts, p6 from spare needle of Left Front Leg, cast on 8 sts, p11 from spare needle of Left Back Leg, cast on 3 sts. *(30 sts)*

Row 2: K14, p1, k15.

Row 3: Inc, p14, k1, p14. *(31 sts)*

Row 4: K14, p1, k16.

Row 5: Inc, p16, k1, p13. *(32 sts)*

Row 6: K13, p1, k18.

Row 7: Inc, p17, k1, p11, p2tog. *(32 sts)*

Row 8: K11, p1, k20.

Row 9: P20, k1, p9, p2tog. *(31 sts)*

Row 10: K9, p1, k21.

Row 11: P22, k1, p6, p2tog. *(30 sts)*

Row 12: K1, p6, k23.

Row 13: P28, p2tog. *(29 sts)*

Row 14: Knit.

Row 15: P9 (hold these 9 sts on spare needle for Neck), p2tog, p16, p2tog. *(18 sts)*

Row 16: Bind off 2 sts, k14 ibos, k2tog. *(15 sts)*

Row 17: Bind off 2 sts, p11 ibos, p2tog. *(12 sts)*

Row 18: Bind off 2 sts, k8 ibos, k2tog. *(9 sts)*

Row 19: Bind off 2 sts, p5 ibos, p2tog. *(6 sts)*
Bind off.

Neck and Head

Row 1: With US 2 (2¾mm) needles and te and em and RS facing, k9 from spare needle of Right Side of Body, then k9 from spare needle of Left Side of Body. *(18 sts)*

Row 2: P4, p2tog, p6, p2tog, p4. *(16 sts)*

Row 3: K4, k2tog, k4, k2tog, k4. *(14 sts)*

Row 4: P2, inc, p8, inc, p2. *(16 sts)*

Row 5: K13, wrap and turn (leave rem 3 sts on left-hand needle unworked).

Row 6: Working top of head on center 10 sts only, p10, w&t.

Row 7: K10, w&t.
Rep last 2 rows once more.

Row 10: P10, w&t.

Head

Bend his legs into shape, and use pipecleaners within his body if you want to manipulate his head.

Row 11: K13. *(16 sts on right-hand needle)*
Row 12: Purl.
Row 13: K12, wrap and turn.
Row 14: P8, w&t.
Row 15: K8, w&t.
Rep last 2 rows once more.
Row 18: P8, w&t.
Row 19: K12. *(16 sts on right-hand needle)*
Row 20: P2, [p2tog] twice, p4, [p2tog] twice, p2. *(12 sts)*
Row 21: K3, k2tog, k2, k2tog, k3. *(10 sts)*
Row 22: P2, p2tog, p2, p2tog, p2. *(8 sts)*
Row 23: [K2tog] 4 times. *(4 sts)*
Bind off.

Tummy

With US 2 (2¾mm) needles and te and em, cast on 8 sts.
Beg with a k row, work 2 rows st st.
Row 3: K2tog, k4, k2tog. *(6 sts)*
Row 4: P2tog, p2, p2tog. *(4 sts)*
Work 8 rows st st.
Row 13: Inc, k2, inc. *(6 sts)*
Work 17 rows st st.
Row 31: K2tog, k2, k2tog. *(4 sts)*
Work 5 rows st st.
Row 37: Inc, k2, inc. *(6 sts)*
Work 7 rows st st.
Join in sn.
Row 45: K2 te and em, k2sn, k2 te and em.
Row 46: P2 te and em, p2sn, p2 te and em.
Row 47: K1 te and em, k4sn, k1 te and em.
Row 48: P1 te and em, p4sn, p1 te and em.
Cont in sn.
Work 4 rows st st.
Row 53: K2tog, k2, k2tog. *(4 sts)*
Work 5 rows st st.
Row 59: [K2tog] twice. *(2 sts)*
Work 2 rows st st.
Bind off.

Ear

(make 2 the same)
With US 2 (2¾mm) needles and te and em, cast on 5 sts.
Work 2 rows st st.
Row 3: K2tog, k1, k2tog. *(3 sts)*
Work 2 rows st st.
Row 6: P3tog and fasten off.

Tail

With US 2 (2¾mm) double-pointed needles and te and em, cast on 8 sts.
Work in i-cord as follows:
Knit 14 rows.
Row 15: K2tog, k4, k2tog. *(6 sts)*
Knit 14 rows.
Row 30: K2tog, k2, k2tog. *(4 sts)*
Knit 3 rows.
Row 34: [K2tog] twice. *(2 sts)*
Row 35: K2tog and fasten off.

To Finish

Sew in ends, leaving ends from bound off rows for sewing up. Using mattress or whip stitch, sew up legs starting at paw. Using mattress or whip stitch, sew along back of cat and down bottom. At head, fold in half and sew bound off edges of nose together. Using mattress or whip stitch, sew cast on row of tummy to bottom end of cat and sew bound off row to nose. Ease and sew tummy to fit body, matching curves to legs. Leave a 1in (2.5cm) gap on one side. Roll two pipecleaners in a small amount of stuffing and bend each one into a U shape. Fold over the ends (so they don't poke out of the paws) and slip into body, one pipecleaner down front legs and one down back legs. Stuff, adding rice or lentils to the tummy for weight, and sew up gap with mattress stitch. Mold into shape as in photograph. Cut a pipecleaner to length of tail, plus a small amount in order to fold over the ends. Slip pipecleaner into tail and sew tail together on the underside. Attach to bottom as in photograph. Sew ears to head, leaving about 3 sts between the two ears. For the eyes, use al yarn to make elongated French knots. Work each knot over 2 sts at a slight angle and wrap the yarn around the needle five times. With bl yarn, make a stitch over the center of the French knot. For whiskers, cut 3in (8cm) strands of sewing thread and thread through cheeks, then trim.

Tortoiseshell Calico Curled Up

This adorable curled up tortie fits neatly into the palm of the hand. When you knit the wrap & turn sections on the body of this cat, you move in one stitch at the beginning of each row, as described in the pattern.

Measurements
Head to tail: 4¾in (12cm)

Materials
- Pair of US 2 (2¾mm) knitting needles
- Pair of US 2 (2¾mm) double-pointed knitting needles
- ¼oz (10g) of Rowan Kidsilk Haze in Ember 644 (em) used DOUBLE throughout
- ¼oz (10g) of Rowan Cashsoft 4ply in Cream 433 (cr)
- ⅛oz (5g) of Rowan Silky Tweed in Tabby 754 (ta)
- Tiny amount of Rowan Cashsoft 4ply in Kiwi 443 (ki) for eyes
- Tiny amount of Rowan Pure Wool 4ply in Black 404 (bl) for pupils
- Tiny amount of Rowan Pure Wool 4ply in Powder 443 (po) for nose
- Rice or lentils for stuffing
- 1 pipecleaner
- Cream sewing thread for whiskers

Abbreviations
See page 141.
See page 141 for Wrap Method.
See page 141 for Intarsia Technique.

Back Leg
With US 2 (2¾mm) needles and cr, cast on 7 sts.
Beg with a k row, work 12 rows st st.
Row 13: Inc, k1, inc, k1, inc, k1, inc. *(11 sts)*
Row 14: Purl.
Row 15: K4, inc, k1, inc, k4. *(13 sts)*
Row 16: Purl.
Row 17: K5, inc, k1, inc, k5. *(15 sts)*
Join in em.
Row 18: P12cr, p3em.
Row 19: K4em, k2cr, inccr, k1cr, inccr, k6cr. *(17 sts)*
Row 20: P10cr, p7em.
Row 21: K7em, incem, k1em, incem, k7cr. *(19 sts)*
Row 22: P5cr, p14em.
Row 23: K15em, k4cr.
Row 24: P2cr, p17em.
Cont in em.
Work 2 rows st st.
Row 27: K7, k2tog, k1, k2tog, k7. *(17 sts)*
Row 28: P6, p2tog, p1, p2tog, p6. *(15 sts)*
Row 29: K5, k2tog, k1, k2tog, k5. *(13 sts)*
Bind off.

Body and Head
(knitted in one piece)
With US 2 (2¾mm) needles and em, cast on 20 sts.
Beg with a k row, work 2 rows st st.
Row 3: K9, inc into next 2 sts, k9. *(22 sts)*
Row 4: Purl.
Row 5: K10, inc into next 2 sts, k10. *(24 sts)*
Row 6: Purl.
Row 7: K11, inc into next 2 sts, k11. *(26 sts)*
Row 8: Purl.
Row 9: K24, wrap and turn.
Row 10: P22, w&t.
Row 11: K10, inc into next 2 sts, k9, w&t. *(23 sts)*
Row 12: P22, w&t.
Join in ta.
Row 13: K6em, k4ta, k4em, k2ta, k5em, w&t. *(21 sts)*
Row 14: P4em, p10ta, p6em, w&t. *(20 sts)*
Row 15: K3em, k6ta, incta into next 2 sts, k7ta, k1em, w&t. *(21 sts)*
Row 16: P6em, p2ta, p2em, p10ta, w&t. *(20 sts)*
Row 17: K5em, k4ta, k2em, k2ta, k6em, w&t. *(19 sts)*
Row 18: P9em, p3ta, p6em, w&t. *(18 sts)*
Row 19: K11em, k3ta, k10em. *(30 sts)*
Join in cr.
Row 20: P2cr, p9em, p3ta, p16em.
Row 21: K2cr, k10em, k2ta, incta into next 2 sts, k4ta, k8em, k2cr. *(32 sts)*
Row 22: P2cr, p7em, p13ta, p7em, p3cr.
Row 23: Inccr, k2cr, k8em, k10ta, k9em, k1cr, inccr. *(34 sts)*
Row 24: P4cr, p10em, p2ta, p2em, p3ta, p9em, p4cr.
Row 25: K5cr, k9em, k3ta, k2em, k2ta, k11em, wrap and turn. *(32 sts)*
Row 26: P17em, p4ta, p6em, p3cr, w&t. *(30 sts)*
Row 27: K4cr, k4em, k5ta, k1em, incem into next 2 sts, k10em, p3cr, w&t. *(31 sts)*
Row 28: P3cr, p17em, p2ta, p5em, p3cr, w&t. *(30 sts)*
Row 29: K4cr, k5em, k2ta, k16em, k2cr, w&t. *(29 sts)*
Row 30: P3cr, p14em, p5ta, p3em, p3cr, w&t. *(28 sts)*
Row 31: K3cr, k3em, k3ta, k16em, k2cr, w&t. *(27 sts)*
Row 32: P3cr, p17em, p2ta, p1em, p3cr, w&t. *(26 sts)*
Row 33: K3cr, k20em, k8cr. *(36 sts)*
Row 34: P9cr, p18em, p9cr.
Row 35: K10cr, k16em, k10cr.

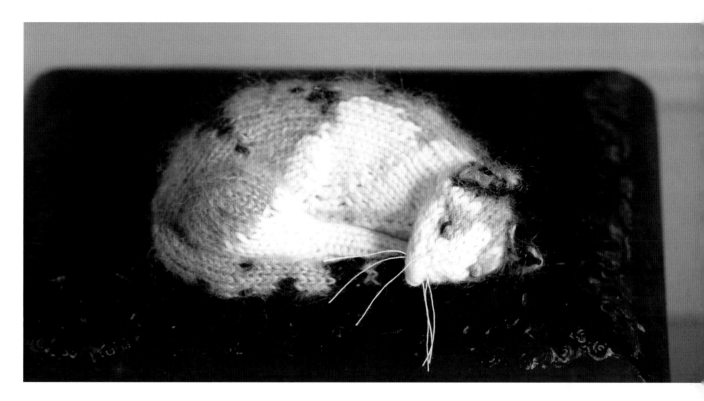

Body

The body can be stuffed with rice or lentils to add weight. When you pick the cat up, he feels as though he is asleep.

Row 36: P10cr, p16em, p10cr.
Row 37: K10cr, k2em, k2ta, k12em, k8cr, wrap and turn. *(34 sts)*
Row 38: P9cr, p10em, p4ta, p1em, p8cr, w&t. *(32 sts)*
Row 39: K8cr, k3em, k4ta, k8em, k8cr, w&t. *(31 sts)*
Row 40: P8cr, p10em, p3ta, p2em, p7cr, w&t. *(30 sts)*
Row 41: K6cr, k3em, k3ta, k1em, [k2togem] twice, k6em, k6cr, w&t. *(27 sts)*
Row 42: P6cr, p10em, p1ta, p4em, p5cr, w&t. *(26 sts)*
Row 43: K6cr, k5em, [k2togem] twice, k5em, k5cr, w&t. *(23 sts)*
Row 44: P3cr, p16em, p3cr, w&t. *(22 sts)*
Row 45: K3cr, k6em, [k2togem] twice, k6em, k8cr. *(30 sts)*
Row 46: P9cr, p12em, p9cr.
Row 47: K2togcr, k8cr, k3em, [k2togem] twice, k3em, k8cr, k2togcr. *(26 sts)*
Row 48: P9cr, p8em, p9cr.
Row 49: K2togcr, k8cr, k1em, [k2togem] twice, k1em, k8cr, k2togcr. *(22 sts)*
Row 50: P2togcr, p7cr, p4em, p7cr, p2tog. *(20 sts)*
Row 51: K2togcr, k6cr, [k2togem] twice, k6cr, k2togcr. *(16 sts)*
Row 52: Purl in cr.
Row 53: K7cr, inccr into next 2 sts, k7cr. *(18 sts)*
Row 54: P8cr, inccr into next 2 sts, p8cr. *(20 sts)*
Row 55: K7cr, k6ta, k3cr, wrap and turn.
Row 56: P2cr, p8ta, p2cr, w&t.
Row 57: K11ta, k1cr, w&t.
Row 58: P11ta, p1cr, w&t.
Row 59: K5ta, k2em, k4ta, k1cr, w&t.
Row 60: P3ta, p6em, p2ta, p1cr, w&t.
Row 61: K2cr, k8em, k6cr. *(20 sts in total)*
Row 62: P8cr, p4em, p8cr.
Row 63: K5cr, k4em, k2cr, k4em, k1cr, wrap and turn.
Row 64: P4em, p2cr, p4em, p2cr, w&t.

Row 65: K2cr, k2em, k4cr, k2em, k2cr, w&t.
Change to cr .
Row 66: P12, w&t.
Row 67: K16. *(20 sts in total)*
Row 68: P2tog, p2, p2tog, p1, p2tog, p2, p2tog, p1, p2tog, p2, p2tog. *(14 sts)*
Row 69: K2, k2tog, k1, [k2tog] twice, k1, k2tog, k2. *(10 sts)*
Row 70: P2, p2tog, p2, p2tog, p2. *(8 sts)*
Row 71: [K2tog] 4 times. *(4 sts)*
Bind off.

Right Ear
With US 2 (2¾mm) needles, cast on 3 sts bl and 1 st em. *(4 sts)*
Row 1: K1em, k3bl.
Row 2: P3bl, p1em.
Row 3: K2togem, k2togbl. *(2 sts)*
Row 4: P1bl, p1em.
Row 5: K2togem and fasten off.

Left Ear
With US 2 (2¾mm) needles, cast on 1 st em and 3 sts bl. *(4 sts)*
Row 1: K3bl, k1em.
Row 2: P1em, p3bl.
Row 3: K2togbl, k2togem. *(2 sts)*
Row 4: P1em, p1bl.
Row 5: K2togem and fasten off.

Tail
With US 2 (2¾mm) double-pointed needles and em, cast on 6 sts.
Work i-cord as follows:
Knit 8 rows.
Join in bl.
Row 9: K2bl, k4em.
With em, knit 4 rows.
Row 14: K2em, k2bl, k2em.
With em, knit 3 rows.
Row 18: K2bl, k4em.
Row 19: K3bl, k3em.
Row 20: K2bl, k4em.

With em, knit 2 rows.
Row 23: K2togbl, k2em, k2togbl. *(4 sts)*
Cont in bl.
Knit 4 rows.
Row 28: K1bl, k2em, k1bl.
Row 29: K1bl, k2em, k1bl.
With bl, knit 2 rows.
Row 32: [K2tog] twice. *(2 sts)*
Row 33: K2tog and fasten off.

To Finish
Sew in ends, leaving ends from bound off rows for sewing up. Using mattress or whip stitch, sew up leg starting at paw. Using mattress or whip stitch, sew along tummy and head, leaving a 1in (2.5cm) gap. Cut a pipecleaner to just longer than cat, fold over the ends, and slip into body and head. The pipecleaner is useful for adding to the curved back and head position. Stuff with rice or lentils to give the sleeping cat more weight, and sew up gap with mattress stitch. Mold into shape. Attach leg and tail as in photograph. With a little stitch, attach the paw and the tip of tail to body. Sew ears to head, leaving about 3 sts between the two ears. For the eyes, use ki yarn to make elongated French knots. Work each knot over 2 sts at a slight angle and wrap the yarn around the needle five times. With bl yarn, make a stitch over the center of the French knot. Using po yarn, embroider a small nose in satin stitch. For whiskers, cut 3in (8cm) strands of sewing thread and thread through cheeks, then trim.

HINTS

Choosing Yarns

Alternative yarns can be used—different colors or thicknesses. If using thicker yarns, refer to the ball band for needle size and use needles at least two sizes smaller than recommended, because the gauge needs to be tight to hold the stuffing. The thicker the yarn, the larger the cat will be. We feel that finer yarns create a more refined cat.

Modifying Patterns

We haven't included all cat breeds, but some can be made with only small adjustments to the patterns. The Munchkin can be knitted from the Siamese pattern, but make the legs much shorter; the Scottish Fold from the Black & White pattern, but with folded over ears set wide on the head; the Manx from the Tabby pattern, but with no tail; and the Bobtail from the British Shorthair pattern, but with a short, fat tail.

Many cat breeds have different markings—mackerel, tabby, tortoiseshell, ticked, calico, white socks, and patches of different colors. Use the pattern for your chosen cat breed with the coloring from another pattern. Some minor adjustments may be needed.

Knitting the Body and Head

When holding stitches to use later on in a pattern, use a spare double-pointed needle. This helps when picking up open stitches, especially from the legs.

Holes can develop around the short-row shaping on the head. When sewing on the ears, use the sewing up end to patch in any holes. Swiss darning can also be used to cover any untidy stitches.

If your cat's neck is rather thick, knit a collar for an instant neck tuck. Alter the length of the tummy section to fit the body of your cat.

If you have knitted a highly patterned cat, using the stranding or Fair Isle technique, the body may be slightly puckered. A light press before sewing up will smooth it out.

Stuffing the Cat

Stuffing the cat is as important as knitting it. Depending on the breed, your cat will need either light, normal, or dense stuffing. For instance, the British Shorthair needs dense stuffing, whereas the Abyssinian's legs need very light stuffing. Refer to the photographs for guidance. We recommend using 100% polyester or kapok stuffing, which is available from craft stores and online retailers. A cat takes ¾–1½oz (20–40g) of stuffing, depending on size.

For the curled up cats, stuff the head and leg with polyester stuffing, then fill the cat's body with rice or lentils. This gives the cat weight, and he will sit neatly in your hand. You can also use lentils in the body of the sitting and lying down cats.

Pipecleaners

The pipecleaners are used to make your cat more stable, and they are also useful for manipulating your cat into poses, such as prowling or sitting down. Add a pipecleaner to the body and into the head of the cat so that you can turn the head.

Tail

Almost all the cats' tails are knitted using double-pointed needles and i-cord. To add shape, cut a pipecleaner to the length of the tail plus 1in (2.5cm), fold over the ends, wrap the tail around the pipecleaner, and sew the edges together. Attach the tail to the body and mold it to the right shape.

Ears

The ears are sewn on with the wrong side facing forward, toward the cat's nose. When sewing on the ears, lightly pinch the ear between your fingers to make a slight curve and then attach it. This should help to stop the ear from turning inside out.

For the ear tufts, unwind some 4ply yarn to make 2ply yarn and cut eight 1in (2.5cm) lengths. Fold two strands in half and use a crochet hook to loop it through the head just in front of the ear. Hook the yarn through and slip the ends through the loop. Pull and trim. Make two sets of tufts for each ear. Use the same method for the tufts on the paws of the Maine Coon, using two strands of mohair.

Eyes

We have used a selection of different eyes for our cats, so use those that most suit your cat. Although we have generally recommended a yarn, you can use any small ends of yarn.

ALMOND EYES
Make an elongated French knot. The knot is worked on the diagonal over 2 sts. Bring the needle out at the required position and wind the yarn around the needle 5 times. Slide the yarn down the needle and reinsert the needle 2 sts away from where it came out. Fasten off. With black yarn, make one elongated stitch over the center of the French knot.

ROUND EYES
Make an elongated French knot as for almond eyes, but reinsert the needle where it came out, making a circle. Catch down the opposite side, creating a flat circle, and fasten off. To make a pupil in the center of the eye, with black yarn make a small French knot.

Nose

All the noses are embroidered using satin stitch. Satin stitch is made up of parallel stitches. Starting at the top of the nose, work two long stitches, tapering to two shorter stitches. Alternatively, you can make a T-shaped nose using two horizontal parallel stitches, with one vertical stitch.

Whiskers

We recommend using six 2in (5cm) lengths of sewing thread or transparent nylon thread, although the latter is not suitable for children and it does tend to slip out.

An Important Note

The cats aren't toys. If you intend to give them to small children, do not use pipecleaners in the construction. Instead, you will need to densely stuff the legs to make the cat stand up.

METHODS

Abbreviations

alt alternate
approx approximately
beg begin(ning)
cm centimeter
cont continue
dec decrease
foll follow(s)(ing)
g grams
ibos including bound off stitch (after binding off the stated number of stitches, one stitch remains on the right-hand needle; this stitch is included in the number of stitches in the following group)
in inches
inc increase (work into front and back of next stitch to increase by one stitch)
k knit
k2(3)tog knit two (three) stitches together
oz ounces
p purl
p2(3)tog purl two (three) stitches together
rem remain(ing)
rep repeat

RS right side
st stitch
st st stockinette stitch
w&t wrap and turn (see Wrap Method below)
WS wrong side
[ ] work instructions within square brackets as directed
* work instructions after/between asterisk(s) as directed

Color Knitting

There are two techniques for working with more than one color in the same row—the intarsia technique and the stranding or Fair Isle technique. For some cats, you can use a combination of both, but here is a guide.

INTARSIA TECHNIQUE
Use this for the Black & White, Ragdoll, Tortoiseshell, Maine Coon, Turkish Van, and Siamese cats.
This method is used when knitting large individual blocks of color. It is best to use a small ball (or long length) for each area of color, otherwise the yarn will become tangled. When changing to a new color, twist the yarns on the wrong side of the work to prevent holes from forming. When starting a new row, turn the knitting so that the yarns hanging from it untwist as much as possible. If you have several colors, you may occasionally have to reorganize the yarns at the back. Your work may look messy in progress, but once the ends are all sewn in, it will look fine.

STRANDING OR FAIR ISLE TECHNIQUE
Use this for the Ginger, Tabby, Abyssinian, and Bengal cats.
If there are no more than four stitches between colors, you can use the stranding or Fair Isle technique. Begin knitting with the first color, then drop this when you introduce the second color. When you come

to the first color again, take it under the second color to twist the yarns. When you come to the second color again, take it over the first color. The secret is not to pull the strands on the wrong side of the work too tightly or the work will pucker.

I-cord

With double-pointed needles, *knit a row. Slide the stitches to the other end of the needle. Do not turn the knitting. Rep from *, pulling the yarn tight on the first st so that the knitting forms a tube.

Wrap Method (w&t)

Knit the number of stitches in the first short row. Slip next stitch purlwise from the left-hand to the right-hand needle. Bring the yarn forward, then slip the stitch back onto the left-hand needle. Return the yarn to the back; this prevents a hole from forming. With this method, you only work on the stated number of sts, leaving some sts unworked at both ends. Use the same method on a purl row, bringing the yarn back and then forward.

Loop Stitch (loop 1)

On a knit row, knit one stitch as normal, but leave the stitch on the left needle. Bring the yarn from the back to the front between the two needles. With the yarn in front, loop the yarn around your left thumb and hold your thumb away from the work to the required length for the loop. The yarn looped around your thumb will measure twice the stated length. Take the yarn back between the two needles to the back of the work. Knit the stitch from the left needle as normal. You now have two stitches on the right-hand needle and a loop between them. Pass the first stitch over the second stitch to trap the loop, which is now secure. The end of the loop can be cut when finishing the cat.

Index of cats

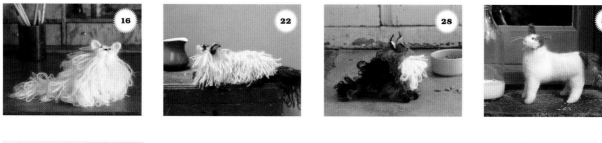

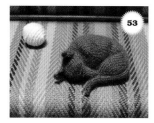

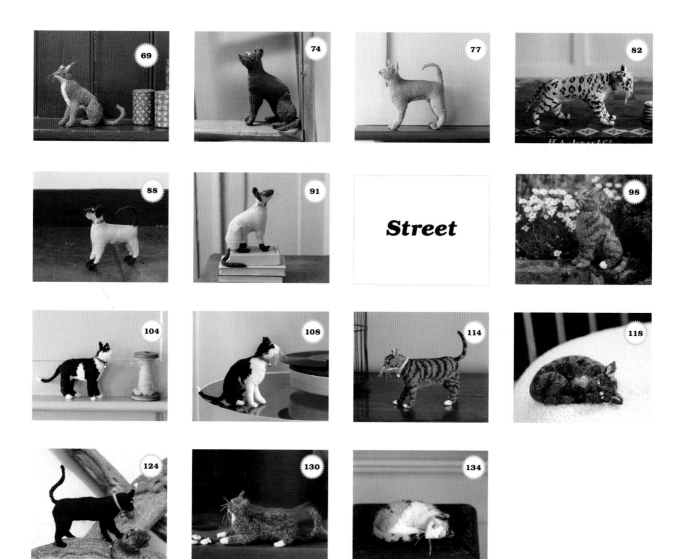

Street

RESOURCES

All of the cats except for the Devon Rex are knitted in Rowan Yarns. For stockists, please refer to their website: www.knitrowan.com The Devon Rex is knitted in silk bouclé, which is available from www.halcyonyarn.com.

Other materials, such as 100% polyester or kapok stuffing, pipecleaners, and cat bells, are available from craft stores and online retailers. A cat takes ¾–1½oz (20–40g) of stuffing, depending on size. For nylon whiskers, use either transparent beading thread or fishing line bought from a fishing tackle shop.

We are selling knitting kits for some of the cats. In each bag, you get a pattern, a pair of knitting needles, the correct amount of yarn, a cat bell, pipecleaners, and the polyester stuffing.

For those who cannot knit but still want a cat, we are selling some of the cats ready-made. You can see the range of cats and kits on our website: www.muirandosborne.co.uk

ACKNOWLEDGMENTS

Thank you to Rowan Yarns again for their generosity.

We are very grateful to the ever vigilant Marilyn Wilson and Kate Haxell for all their hard work. Many thanks to Caroline Dawnay and Olivia Hunt for being so helpful and encouraging. We would also like to thank Katie Cowan for sticking with us, and Amy Christian and everyone at Collins & Brown for being so enthusiastic, and to Holly Jolliffe for more marvellous photographs.

Finally, a special thank you to Shan Lancaster and Caroline Kington.

THE AUTHORS

Sally Muir and Joanna Osborne run their own knitwear business, Muir and Osborne. They sell their knitwear to stores in the United States, United Kingdom, Europe, and Japan. Several pieces of their knitwear are in the permanent collection at the Victoria and Albert Museum, London. *Knit Your Own Cat* is the follow-up to the bestselling *Knit Your Own Dog*.